THE WOMAN QUESTION

The
WOMAN QUESTION

Selections from the Writings of

KARL MARX

FREDERICK ENGELS

V. I. LENIN

JOSEPH STALIN

INTERNATIONAL PUBLISHERS, NEW YORK

CONTENTS

EDITOR'S PREFACE

This book is a collection of excerpts from the writings of Marx, Engels, Lenin, and Stalin on the position of women in society. It contains selections from their major works, as well as articles and speeches. Taken together, these present the essence and scope of the woman question, as developed by the leading exponents of scientific socialism.

The first part of the book takes up the origin of the woman question and explains how it became a special question. Here the reader will find selections from Engels' *Origin of the Family* which analyze the historical development of the family, the reasons for changes in the relations of the sexes, and the evolution of morals.

Subsequent chapters take up the economic, political, and social status of women under both capitalism and socialism. Selections from Marx's *Capital* and Engels' *Condition of the Working Class in England in 1844* examine the factors that drew women into capitalist production, the relation of women to production as shown by employment, wages, and working conditions in the early factories, and the effect of women's employment on family and children.

Excerpts from Lenin's writings in particular deal with capitalist and socialist morality, contrasting and analyzing the two. Personal relationships between men and women, questions of marriage and divorce, and the hypocrisy of bourgeois attitudes toward family life are discussed in their theoretical and practical aspects. Other selections show the limitations of purely legal equality for women, and explain the further conditions necessary for complete emancipation of women.

7

Selections from Lenin and Stalin define the problems of drawing women into full productive, political, and social life under socialism and show how they are solved in the Soviet Union.

The Appendix presents a portion of Lenin's famous interview with Clara Zetkin, in which they discussed the status of women in the new Soviet state and in the capitalist countries as well.

For the reader who wishes to pursue the subject further, there is a bibliography of the works of Marx, Engels, Lenin, and Stalin in which these selections appear.

As a whole, the book is a guide to understanding the role and position of women today. Taken with current writings on the subject, it provides both historical perspective and theoretical insight into the tremendous force for peace and progress which women can become.

I. The Enslavement of Women

1. MEN, WOMEN, AND DIVISION OF LABOR

History teaches us that the class or social group which plays the principal role in social production and performs the main functions in production must, in the course of time, inevitably take control of that production. There was a time, under the matriarchate, when women were regarded as the controllers of production. Why was this? Because under the kind of production then prevailing, primitive agriculture, women played the principal role in production, they performed the main functions, while the men roamed the forests in quest of game. Then came the time, under the patriarchate, when the predominant position in production passed to men. Why did this change take place? Because under the kind of production prevailing at that time, stockbreeding, in which the principal instruments of production were the spear, the lasso, and the bow and arrow, the principal role was played by men.

Stalin, *Anarchism or Socialism?*

The increase of production in all branches—cattle-raising, agriculture, domestic handicrafts—gave human labor-power the capacity to produce a larger product than was necessary for its maintenance. At the same time it increased the daily amount of work to be done by each member of the gens, household community, or single family. It was now desirable to bring in new labor forces. War provided them; prisoners of war were turned into slaves. With its increase of the productivity of labor, and therefore of wealth, and its extension of the field of production, the first great social division of

9

labor was bound, in the general historical conditions prevailing, to bring slavery in its train. From the first great social division of labor arose the first great cleavage of society into two classes: masters and slaves, exploiters and exploited.

As to how and when the herds passed out of the common possession of the tribe or the gens into the ownership of individual heads of families, we know nothing at present. But in the main it must have occurred during this stage. With the herds and the other new riches, a revolution came over the family. To procure the necessities of life had always been the business of the man: he produced and owned the means of doing so. The herds were the new means of producing these necessities; the taming of the animals in the first instance and their later tending were the man's work. To him, therefore, belonged the cattle, and to him the commodities and the slaves received in exchange for cattle. All the surplus which the acquisition of the necessities of life now yielded fell to the man; the woman shared in its enjoyment, but had no part in its ownership. The "savage" warrior and hunter had been content to take second place in the house, after the woman; the "gentler" shepherd, in the arrogance of his wealth, pushed himself forward into the first place and the woman down into the second. And she could not complain. The division of labor within the family had regulated the division of property between the man and the woman. That division of labor had remained the same; and yet it now turned the previous domestic relation upside down, simply because the division of labor outside the family had changed. The same cause which had ensured to the woman her previous supremacy in the house—that her activity was confined to domestic labor—this same cause now ensured the man's supremacy in the house: the domestic labor of the woman no longer counted beside the acquisition of the necessities of life by the man; the latter was everything, the former an unimportant extra. We can already see from this that to emancipate woman and make her the equal of man is and remains an impossibility so long as the woman is shut out from social productive labor and restricted to private domestic labor. The emancipation of woman will only be possible when woman can take part in production on a large, social scale, and domestic work no longer claims anything but an insignificant amount of her time. And only now has that become possible through modern large-scale industry, which does not merely permit of the employment of female labor over a wide range, but positively demands it, while it also tends towards ending private domestic labor by changing it more and more into a public industry.

The man now being actually supreme in the house, the last barrier to his absolute supremacy had fallen. This autocracy was confirmed and perpetuated by the overthrow of mother-right, the introduction of father-right, and the gradual transition of the pairing marriage into monogamy.

Engels, *Origin of the Family.*

2. THE PAIRING FAMILY

The history of the family in primitive times consists in the progressive narrowing of the circle, originally embracing the whole tribe, within which the two sexes have a common conjugal relation. The continuous exclusion, first of nearer, then of more and more remote relatives, and at last even of relatives by marriage, ends by making any kind of group marriage practically impossible. Finally, there remains only the single, still loosely linked pair, the molecule with whose dissolution marriage itself ceases. This in itself shows what a small part individual sex-love, in the modern sense of the word, played in the rise of monogamy. Yet stronger proof is afforded by the practice of all peoples at this stage of development. Whereas in the earlier forms of the family men never lacked women, but, on the contrary, had too many rather than too few, women had now become scarce and highly sought after. Hence it is with the pairing marriage that there begins the capture and purchase of women—widespread *symptoms,* but no more than symptoms, of the much deeper change that had occurred. These symptoms, mere methods of procuring wives, the pedantic Scot, McLennan, has transmogrified into special classes of families under the names of "marriage by capture" and "marriage by purchase." In general, whether among the American Indians or other peoples (at the same stage), the conclusion of a marriage is the affair not of the two parties concerned, who are often not consulted at all, but of their mothers. Two persons entirely unknown to each other are often thus affianced; they only learn that the bargain has been struck when the time for marrying approaches. Before the wedding the bridegroom gives presents to the bride's gentile relatives (to those on the mother's side, therefore, not to the father and his relations), which are regarded as gift payments in return for the girl. The marriage is still terminable at the desire of either partner, but among many tribes, the Iroquois, for example, public opinion has gradually developed against such separations; when differences arise between husband and wife, the gens relatives of both partners act as mediators, and only if these efforts prove fruitless does a separation take place, the wife then keeping the children and each partner being free to marry again.

The pairing family, itself too weak and unstable to make an independent household necessary or even desirable, in no wise destroys the communistic household inherited from earlier times. Communistic housekeeping, however, means the supremacy of women in the house; just as the exclusive recognition of the female parent, owing to the impossibility of recognizing the male parent with certainty, means that the women—the mothers—are held in high respect. One of the most absurd notions taken over from eighteenth-century enlightenment is that in the beginning of society woman was the slave of man. Among all savages and all barbarians of the lower and middle stages, and to a certain extent of the upper stage also, the position of women is not only free, but honorable. As to what it still is in the pairing marriage, let us hear the evidence of Ashur Wright, for many years missionary among the Iroquois Senecas:

"As to their family system, when occupying the old longhouses [communistic households comprising several families], it is probable that some one clan [gens] predominated, the women taking in husbands, however, from the other clans [gentes]. . . . Usually, the female portion ruled the house. . . . The stores were in common; but woe to the luckless husband or lover who was too shiftless to do his share of the providing. No matter how many children, or whatever goods he might have in the house, he might at any time be ordered to pick up his blanket and budge; and after such orders it would not be healthful for him to attempt to disobey. The house would be too hot for him; and . . . he must retreat to his own clan [gens]; or, as was often done, go and start a new matrimonial alliance in some other. The women were the great power among the clans [gentes], as everywhere else. They did not hesitate, when occasion required, 'to knock off the horns' as it was technically called, from the head of a chief, and send him back to the ranks of the warriors."*

The communistic household, in which most or all of the women belong to one and the same gens, while the men come from various gentes, is the material foundation of that supremacy of the women which was general in primitive times. . . . The reports of travelers and missionaries, I may add, to the effect that women among savages and barbarians are overburdened with work in no way contradict what has been said. The division of labor between the two sexes is determined by quite other causes than by the position of woman in society. Among peoples where the women have to work far harder than we think suitable, there is often much more real respect for women than among our Europeans. The lady of civilization, surrounded by false homage and estranged from all real work, has an infinitely lower social position than the hard-working woman of barbarism, who was regarded among her people as a real lady (lady, *frowa, Frau*—mistress) and who was also a lady in character.

Engels, *Origin of the Family.*

* Quoted by Morgan in *Ancient Society*, Chicago, 1907, p. 464.—*Ed.*

3. THE END OF MOTHER-RIGHT

Up to the lower stage of barbarism, permanent wealth had consisted almost solely of house, clothing, crude ornaments, and the tools for obtaining and preparing food—boat, weapons, and domestic utensils of the simplest kind. Food had to be won afresh day by day. Now, with their herds of horses, camels, asses, cattle, sheep, goats, and pigs, the advancing pastoral peoples—the Semites on the Euphrates and the Tigris, and the Aryans in the Indian country of the Five Streams (Punjab), in the Ganges region, and in the steppes, then much more abundantly watered, of the Oxus and the Jaxartes—had acquired property which only needed supervision and the rudest care to reproduce itself in steadily increasing quantities and to supply the most abundant food in the form of milk and meat. All former means of procuring food now receded into the background; hunting, formerly a necessity, now became a luxury.

But to whom did this new wealth belong? Originally to the gens, without a doubt. Private property in herds must have already started at an early period, however. It is difficult to say whether the author of the so-called first book of Moses regarded the patriarch Abraham as the owner of his herds in his own right as head of a family community or by right of his position as actual hereditary head of a gens. What is certain is that we must not think of him as a property owner in the modern sense of the word. And it is also certain that at the threshold of authentic history we already find the herds everywhere separately owned by heads of families, as are the artistic products of barbarism—metal implements, luxury articles and, finally, the human cattle—the slaves.

For now slavery had also been invented. To the barbarian of the lower stage, a slave was valueless. Hence the treatment of defeated enemies by the American Indians was quite different from that at a higher stage. The men were killed or adopted as brothers into the tribe of the victors; the women were taken as wives or otherwise adopted with their surviving children. At this stage human labor-power still does not produce any considerable surplus over and above its maintenance costs. That was no longer the case after the introduction of cattle-breeding, metal-working, weaving and, lastly, agriculture. Just as the wives whom it had formerly been so easy to obtain had now acquired an exchange value and were bought, so also with the forces of labor, particularly since the herds had definitely become family possessions. The family did not multiply so rapidly as the cattle. More people were needed to look after them; for this purpose use could be made of the enemies captured in war, who could also be bred just as easily as the cattle themselves.

Once it had passed into the private possession of families and there rapidly begun to augment, this wealth dealt a severe blow to the society founded on pairing marriage and the matriarchal gens. Pairing marriage had brought a new element into the family. By the side of the natural mother of the child it placed its natural and attested father, with a better warrant of paternity, probably, than that of many a "father" today. According to the division of labor within the family at that time, it was the man's part to obtain food and the instruments of labor necessary for the purpose. He therefore also owned the instruments of labor, and in the event of husband and wife separating, he took them with him, just as she retained her household goods. Therefore, according to the social custom of the time, the man was also the owner of the new source of subsistence, the cattle, and later of the new instruments of labor, the slaves. But according to the custom of the same society, his children could not inherit from him. For as regards inheritance, the position was as follows:

At first, according to mother-right—so long, therefore, as descent was reckoned only in the female line—and according to the original custom of inheritance within the gens, the gentile relatives inherited from a deceased fellow member of their gens. His property had to remain within the gens. His effects being insignificant, they probably always passed in practice to his nearest gentile relations—that is, to his blood relations on the mother's side. The children of the dead man, however, did not belong to his gens, but to that of their mother; it was from her that they inherited, at first conjointly with her other blood-relations, later perhaps with rights of priority; they could not inherit from their father, because they did not belong to his gens, within which his property had to remain. When the owner of the herds died, therefore, his herds would go first to his brothers and sisters and to his sister's children, or to the issue of his mother's sisters. But his own children were disinherited.

Thus, on the one hand, in proportion as wealth increased, it made the man's position in the family more important than the woman's, and on the other hand created an impulse to exploit this strengthened position in order to overthrow, in favor of his children, the traditional order of inheritance. This, however, was impossible so long as descent was reckoned according to mother-right. Mother-right, therefore, had to be overthrown, and overthrown it was. This was by no means so difficult as it looks to us today. For this revolution—one of the most decisive ever experienced by humanity—could take place without disturbing a single one of the living members of a gens. All could remain as they were. A simple decree sufficed that in the future the offspring of the male members should remain within the gens, but that of the female should be excluded by being transferred to the gens of their father. The reckoning of descent in the female line and the matri-archal law of inheritance were thereby overthrown, and the male line of descent and the paternal law of inheritance were substituted for them. As to how and when this revolution took place among civilized peoples, we have no knowledge. It falls entirely within prehistoric times. . . .

The overthrow of mother-right was the *world historical defeat of the female sex*. The man took command in the home also; the woman was degraded and reduced to servi-tude, she became the slave of his lust and a mere instrument for the production of children. This degraded position of the woman, especially conspicuous among the Greeks of the heroic and still more of the classical age, has gradually been palliated and glossed over, and sometimes clothed in a milder form; in no sense has it been abolished.

Engels, *Origin of the Family.*

4. THE MONOGAMOUS FAMILY

It develops out of the pairing family, as previously shown, in the transitional period between the upper and middle stages of barbarism; its decisive victory is one of the signs that civilization is beginning. It is based on the supremacy of the man, the express purpose being to produce children of undisputed paternity; such paternity is demanded because these children are later to come into their father's property as his natural heirs. It is distinguished from pairing marriage by the much greater strength of the marriage tie, which can no longer be dissolved at either partner's wish. As a rule, it is now only the man who can dissolve it, and put away his wife. The right of conjugal infidelity also remains secured to him, at any rate by custom (the *Code Napoléon* explicitly accords it to the husband as long as he does not bring his concubine into the house), and as social life develops he exercises his right more and more; should the wife recall the old form of sexual life and attempt to revive it, she is punished more severely than ever.

We meet this new form of the family in all its severity among the Greeks. While the position of the goddesses in their mythology, as Marx points out, brings before us an earlier period when the position of women was freer and more respected, in the heroic age we find the woman already being humiliated by the domination of the man and by competition from girl slaves. Note how Telemachus in the *Odyssey* silences his mother.* In Homer young women are booty and are handed over to the pleasure of the conquerors, the handsomest being picked by the commanders in order of rank;

* The reference is to a passage where Telemachus, son of Odysseus and Penelope, tells his mother to get on with her weaving and leave the men to mind their own business (*Odyssey*, Book 21, ll. 350 ff.).—*Ed.*

the entire *Iliad,* it will be remembered, turns on the quarrel of Achilles and Agamemnon over one of these slaves. If a hero is of any importance, Homer also mentions the captive girl with whom he shares his tent and his bed. These girls were also taken back to Greece and brought under the same roof as the wife, as Cassandra was brought by Agamemnon in Aeschylus; the sons begotten of them received a small share of the paternal inheritance and had the full status of freemen. Teucer, for instance, is a natural son of Telamon by one of these slaves and has the right to use his father's name.

The legitimate wife was expected to put up with all this, but herself to remain strictly chaste and faithful. In the heroic age a Greek woman is, indeed, more respected than in the period of civilization, but to her husband she is after all nothing but the mother of his legitimate children and heirs, his chief housekeeper and the supervisor of his female slaves, whom he can and does take as concubines if he so fancies. It is the existence of slavery side by side with monogamy, the presence of young, beautiful slaves belonging unreservedly to the *man,* that stamps monogamy from the very beginning with its specific character of monogamy *for the woman only,* but not for the man. And that is the character it still has today.

Coming to the later Greeks, we must distinguish between Dorians and Ionians. Among the former—Sparta is the classic example—marriage relations are in some ways still more archaic than even in Homer. The recognized form of marriage in Sparta was a pairing marriage, modified according to the Spartan conceptions of the state, in which there still survived vestiges of group marriage. Childless marriages were dissolved; King Anaxandridas (about 650 B.C.), whose first wife was childless, took a second and kept two households; about the same time, King Ariston, who had two unfruitful wives, took a third, but dismissed one of the other two. On the other hand, several brothers could have a wife in common; a friend who preferred his friend's wife could share her with him; and it was considered quite proper to place one's wife at the disposal of a sturdy "stallion," as Bismarck would say, even if he was not a citizen. A passage in Plutarch, where a Spartan woman refers an importunate wooer to her husband, seems to indicate, according to Schömann, even greater freedom. Real adultery, secret infidelity by the woman without the husband's knowledge, was therefore unheard of. On the other hand, domestic slavery was unknown in Sparta, at least during its best period; the unfree helots were segregated on the estates and the Spartans were therefore less tempted to take the helots' wives. Inevitably in these conditions women held a much more honored position in Sparta than anywhere else in Greece. The Spartan women and the élite of the Athenian *hetairai* are the only Greek women of whom the ancients speak with respect and whose words they thought it worth while to record.

The position is quite different among the Ionians; here Athens is typical. Girls only learned spinning, weaving, and sewing, and at most a little reading and writing. They lived more or less behind locked doors and had no company except other women. The women's apartments formed a separate part of the house, on the upper floor or at the back, where men, especially strangers, could not easily enter, and to which the women retired when men visited the house. They never went out without being accompanied by a female slave; indoors they were kept under regular guard. Aristophanes speaks of Molossian dogs kept to frighten away adulterers, and, at any rate in the Asiatic towns, eunuchs were employed to keep watch over the women—making and exporting eunuchs was an industry in Chios as early as Herodotus' time, and, according to Wachsmuth, it was not only the barbarians who bought the supply. In Euripides a woman is called an *oikourema*, a thing (the word is neuter) for looking after the house, and, apart from her business of bearing children, that was all she was for the Athenian—his chief female domestic servant. The man had his athletics and his public business, from which women were barred; in addition, he often had female slaves at his disposal and during the most flourishing days of Athens an extensive system of prostitution which the state at least favored. It was precisely through this system of prostitution that the only Greek women of personality were able to develop, and to acquire that intellectual and artistic culture by which they stand out as high above the general level of classical womanhood as the Spartan women by their qualities of character. But that a woman had to be a *hetaira* before she could be a woman is the worst condemnation of the Athenian family.

This Athenian family became in time the accepted model for domestic relations, not only among the Ionians, but to an increasing extent among all the Greeks of the mainland and colonies also. But, in spite of locks and guards, Greek women found plenty of opportunity for deceiving their husbands. The men, who would have been ashamed to show any love for their wives, amused themselves by all sorts of love affairs with *hetairai;* but this degradation of the women was avenged on the men and degraded them also, till they fell into the abominable practice of sodomy and degraded alike their gods and themselves with the myth of Ganymede.

This is the origin of monogamy as far as we can trace it back among the most civilized and highly developed people of antiquity. It was not in any way the fruit of individual sex-love, with which it had nothing whatever to do; marriages remained as before marriages of convenience. It was the first form of the family to be based, not on natural, but on economic conditions—on the victory of private property over primitive, natural communal property. The Greeks themselves put the matter quite frankly: the sole exclusive aims of monogamous marriage were to make the man supreme in the family, and to propagate, as the future heirs to his wealth, children indisputably his own. Otherwise, marriage was a burden, a duty which had to be performed, whether one liked it or not, to gods, state, and one's ancestors. In Athens the law exacted from the man not only marriage but also the performance of a minimum of so-called conjugal duties.

Thus when monogamous marriage first makes its appearance in history, it is not as the reconciliation of man and woman, still less as the highest form of such a reconciliation. Quite the contrary. Monogamous marriage comes on the scene as the subjugation of the one sex by the other; it announces a struggle between the sexes unknown throughout the whole previous prehistoric period. In an old unpublished manuscript, written by Marx and myself in 1846,* I find the words: "The first division of labor is that between man and woman for the propagation of children." And today I can add: The first class opposition that appears in history coincides with the development of the antagonism between man and woman in monogamous marriage, and the first class oppression coincides with that of the female sex by the male. Monogamous marriage was a great historical step forward; nevertheless, together with slavery and private wealth, it opens the period that has lasted until today in which every step forward is also relatively a step backward, in which prosperity and development for some is won through the misery and frustration of others. It is the cellular form of civilized society, in which the nature of the oppositions and contradictions fully active in that society can be already studied.

The old comparative freedom of sexual intercourse by no means disappeared with the victory of pairing marriage or even of monogamous marriage:

"The old conjugal system, now reduced to narrower limits by the gradual disappearance of the punaluan groups, still environed the advancing family, which it was to follow to the verge of civilization. . . . It finally disappeared in the new form of hetaerism, which still follows mankind in civilization as a dark shadow upon the family."†

By "hetaerism" Morgan understands the practice, *coexistent with monogamous marriage,* of sexual intercourse between men and unmarried women outside marriage, which, as we know, flourishes in the most varied forms throughout the whole period of civilization and develops more and more into open prostitution. This hetaerism derives quite directly from group marriage, from the ceremonial surrender by

---

* The reference here is to *The German Ideology,* written by Marx and Engels in Brussels in 1845-46 and first published in 1932 by the Marx-Engels-Lenin Institute in Moscow. See *The German Ideology,* New York, 1939, p. 20.—*Ed.*
† Morgan, *op. cit.,* p. 511.—*Ed.*

which women purchased the right of chastity. Surrender for money was at first a religious act; it took place in the temple of the goddess of love, and the money originally went into the temple treasury. The temple slaves of Anaitis in Armenia and of Aphrodite in Corinth, like the sacred dancing girls attached to the temples of India, the so-called *bayaderes* (the word is a corruption of the Portuguese word *bailadeira*, meaning female dancer), were the first prostitutes. Originally the duty of every woman, this surrender was later performed by these priestesses alone as representatives of all other women. Among other peoples, hetaerism derives from the sexual freedom allowed to girls before marriage—again, therefore, a relic of group marriage, but handed down in a different way. With the rise of the inequality of property—already at the upper stage of barbarism, therefore—wage-labor appears sporadically side by side with slave labor, and at the same time, as its necessary correlate, the professional prostitution of free women side by side with the forced surrender of the slave. Thus the heritage which group marriage has bequeathed to civilization is double-edged, just as everything civilization brings forth is double-edged, double-tongued, divided against itself, contradictory: here monogamy, there hetaerism, with its most extreme form, prostitution. For hetaerism is as much a social institution as any other; it continues the old sexual freedom—to the advantage of the men. Actually not merely tolerated, but gaily practiced, by the ruling classes particularly, it is condemned in words. But in reality this condemnation never falls on the men concerned, but only on the women; they are despised and outcast, in order that the unconditional supremacy of men over the female sex may be once more proclaimed as a fundamental law of society.

But a second contradiction thus develops within monogamous marriage itself. At the side of the husband who embellishes his existence with hetaerism stands the neglected wife. And one cannot have one side of this contradiction without the other, any more than a man has a whole apple in his hand after eating half. But that seems to have been the husbands' notion, until their wives taught them better. With monogamous marriage, two constant social types, unknown hitherto, make their appearance on the scene—the wife's attendant lover and the cuckold husband. The husbands had won the victory over the wives, but the vanquished magnanimously provided the crown. Together with monogamous marriage and hetaerism, adultery became an unavoidable social institution—denounced, severely penalized, but impossible to suppress. At best, the certain paternity of the children rested on moral conviction as before, and to solve the insoluble contradiction the *Code Napoléon*, Art. 312, decreed: *"L'enfant conçu pendant le mariage a pour père le mari,"* the father of a child conceived during marriage is—the husband. Such is the final result of three thousand years of monogamous marriage.

Thus, wherever the monogamous family remains true to its historical origin and clearly reveals the antagonism between the man and the woman expressed in the man's exclusive supremacy, it exhibits in miniature the same oppositions and contradictions as those in which society has been moving, without power to resolve or overcome them, ever since it split into classes at the beginning of civilization. I am speaking here, of course, only of those cases of monogamous marriage where matrimonial life actually proceeds according to the original character of the whole institution, but where the wife rebels against the husband's supremacy. Not all marriages turn out thus, as nobody knows better than the German philistine, who can no more assert his rule in the home than he can in the state, and whose wife, with every right, wears the trousers he is unworthy of. But, to make up for it, he considers himself far above his French companion in misfortune, to whom, oftener than to him, something much worse happens.

However, monogamous marriage did not by any means appear always and everywhere in the classically harsh form it took among the Greeks. Among the Romans, who, as future world conquerors, had a larger, if a less fine, vision than the Greeks, women were freer and more respected. A

Roman considered that his power of life and death over his wife sufficiently guaranteed her conjugal fidelity. Here, moreover, the wife equally with the husband could dissolve the marriage at will. But the greatest progress in the development of individual marriage certainly came with the entry of the Germans into history, and for the reason that the Germans—on account of their poverty, very probably—were still at a stage where monogamy seems not yet to have become perfectly distinct from pairing marriage. We infer this from three facts mentioned by Tacitus. First, though marriage was held in great reverence—"they content themselves with one wife, the women live hedged round with chastity"—polygamy was the rule for the distinguished members and the leaders of the tribe, a condition of things similar to that among the Americans, where pairing marriage was the rule. Secondly, the transition from mother-right to father-right could only have been made a short time previously, for the brother on the mother's side—the nearest gentile male relation according to mother-right—was still considered almost closer of kin than the father, corresponding again to the standpoint of the American Indians, among whom Marx, as he often said, found the key to the understanding of our own primitive age. And, thirdly, women were greatly respected among the Germans, and also influential in public affairs, which is in direct contradiction to the supremacy of men in monogamy. In almost all these points the Germans agree with the Spartans, among whom also, as we saw, pairing marriage had not yet been completely overcome. Thus, here again an entirely new influence came to power in the world with the Germans. The new monogamy, which now developed from the mingling of peoples amid the ruins of the Roman world, clothed the supremacy of the men in milder forms and gave women a position which, outwardly at any rate, was much more free and respected than it had ever been in classical antiquity. Only now were the conditions realized in which through monogamy—within it, parallel to it, or in opposition to it, as the case might be—the greatest moral advance we owe to it could be achieved: modern individual sex-love, which had hitherto been unknown to the entire world.

This advance, however, undoubtedly sprang from the fact that the Germans still lived in pairing families and grafted the corresponding position of women onto the monogamous system, so far as that was possible. It most decidedly did not spring from the legendary virtue and wonderful moral purity of the German character, which was nothing more than the freedom of the pairing family from the crying moral contradictions of monogamy. On the contrary, in the course of their migrations the Germans had morally much deteriorated, particularly during their southeasterly wanderings among the nomads of the Black Sea steppes, from whom they acquired, not only equestrian skill, but also gross, unnatural vices, as Ammianus expressly states of the Taifalians and Procopius of the Herulians.

But if monogamy was the only one of all the known forms of the family through which modern sex-love could develop, that does not mean that within monogamy modern sexual love developed exclusively or even chiefly as the love of husband and wife for each other. That was precluded by the very nature of strictly monogamous marriage under the rule of the man. Among all historically active classes—that is, among all ruling classes—matrimony remained what it had been since the pairing marriage, a matter of convenience which was arranged by the parents. The first historical form of sexual love as passion, a passion recognized as natural to all human beings (at least if they belonged to the ruling classes), and as the highest form of the sexual impulse—and that is what constitutes its specific character—this first form of individual sexual love, the chivalrous love of the Middle Ages, was by no means conjugal. Quite the contrary. In its classic form among the Provençals, it heads straight for adultery, and the poets of love celebrated adultery. The flower of Provençal love poetry are the Albas (*aubades,* songs of dawn). They describe in glowing colors how the knight lies in bed beside his love—the wife of another man—while outside stands the watchman who calls to him as soon as the first gray of dawn (*alba*) appears, so that he can get away unobserved; the parting scene then forms the climax of the poem. The northern French and also the worthy Germans adopted this kind of poetry together with the corresponding fashion of chivalrous love; old Wolfram of Eschenbach has left us three wonderfully beautiful songs of dawn on this same improper subject, which I like better than his three long heroic poems.

Engels, *Origin of the Family.*

II. The Exploitation of Women

1. DEATH FROM OVERWORK

In the last week of June 1863, all the London daily papers published a paragraph with the "sensational" heading: "Death from simple overwork." It dealt with the death of the milliner, Mary Anne Walkley, twenty years of age, employed in a highly respectable dressmaking establishment, exploited by a lady with the pleasant name of Elise.

The old, often-told story was once more recounted. This girl worked, on an average, sixteen and a half hours, during the season often thirty hours, without a break, whilst her failing labor-power was revived by occasional supplies of sherry, port, or coffee. It was just now the height of the season. It was necessary to conjure up in the twinkling of an eye the gorgeous dresses for the noble ladies bidden to the ball in honor of the newly imported Princess of Wales.

Mary Anne Walkley had worked without intermission for twenty-six and a half hours, with sixty other girls, thirty in one room that only afforded one-third of the cubic feet of air required for them. At night they slept in pairs in one of the stifling holes into which the bedroom was divided by partitions of board. And this was one of the best millinery establishments in London. Mary Anne Walkley fell ill on the Friday, died on Sunday, without, to the astonishment of Madame Elise, having previously completed the work in hand.

The doctor, Mr. Keys, called too late to the death bed, duly bore witness before the coroner's jury that: "Mary Anne Walkley had died from long hours of work in an overcrowded workroom, and a too small and badly ventilated bedroom."

In order to give the doctor a lesson in good manners, the coroner's jury thereupon brought in a verdict that "the deceased had died of apoplexy, but there was reason to fear that her death had been accelerated by overwork in an overcrowded workroom, etc."

"Our white slaves," cried the *Morning Star*, the organ of the free-traders, Cobden and Bright, "our white slaves, who are toiled into the grave, for the most part silently pine and die."

Marx, *Capital*. Vol. I.

2. CHEAP LABOR

Before the labor of women and of children under ten years of age was forbidden in mines, capitalists considered the employment of naked women and girls, often in company with men, so far sanctioned by their moral code, and especially by their ledgers, that it was only after the passing of the Act that they had recourse to machinery. The Yankees have invented a stonebreaking machine. The English do not make use of it, because the "wretch" (the recognized term in English political economy for the agricultural laborer) who does this work gets paid for such a small portion of his labor that machinery would increase the cost of production to the capitalist. In England women are still occasionally used instead of horses for hauling canal boats, because the labor required to produce horses and machines is an accurately known quantity, while that required to maintain the women of the surplus population is below all calculation.

Marx, *Capital*, Vol. I.

In so far as machinery dispenses with muscular power, it becomes a means of employing laborers of slight muscular strength, and those whose bodily development is incomplete, but whose limbs are all the more supple. The labor of women and children was, therefore, the first thing sought for by capitalists who used machinery. That mighty substitute for labor and laborers was forthwith changed into a means for increasing the number of wage-laborers by enrolling, under the direct sway of capital, every member of the workman's family, without distinction of age or sex. Compulsory work for the capitalist usurped the place, not only of the children's play, but also of free labor at home within moderate limits for the support of the family.

The value of labor-power was determined, not only by the labor-time necessary to maintain the individual adult laborer, but also by that necessary to maintain his family. Machinery, by throwing every member of that family on to the labor market, spreads the value of the man's labor-power over his whole family. It thus depreciates his labor-power. To purchase the labor-power of a family of four workers may, perhaps, cost more than it formerly did to purchase the labor-power of the head of the family, but, in return, four days' labor takes the place of one, and their price falls in proportion to the excess of the surplus labor of four over the surplus labor of one. In order that the family may live, four people must now not only labor but expend surplus labor for the capitalist. Thus we see that machinery, while augmenting the human material that forms the principal object of capital's exploiting power, at the same time raises the degree of exploitation.

Marx, *Capital*, Vol. I.

3. EXPLOITATION OF CHILDREN

So long as factory legislation is confined to regulating the labor in factories, manufactures, etc., it is regarded as a mere interference with the exploiting rights of capital. But when it comes to regulating the so-called "home-labor,"* it is immediately viewed as a direct attack on the *patria potestas*, on parental authority. The tender-hearted English Parliament long affected to shrink from taking this step. The force

---

* This sort of labor goes on mostly in small workshops, as we have seen in the lace-making and straw-plaiting trades, and as could be shown more in detail from the metal trades of Sheffield, Birmingham, etc.

of facts, however, compelled it at last to acknowledge that modern industry, in overturning the economical foundation on which was based the traditional family, and the family labor corresponding to it, had also unloosened all traditional family ties. The rights of the children had to be proclaimed. The final report of the Commission of 1866, states: "It is unhappily, to a painful degree, apparent throughout the whole of the evidence, that against no persons do the children of both sexes so much require protection as against their parents." The system of unlimited exploitation of childrens' labor in general and the so-called home-labor in particular is "maintained only because the parents are able, without check or control, to exercise this arbitrary and mischievous power over their young and tender offspring. . . . Parents must not possess the absolute power of making their children mere 'machines to earn so much weekly wage.' . . . The children and young persons, therefore, in all such cases may justifiably claim from the legislature, as a natural right, that an exemption should be secured to them from what destroys prematurely their physical strength and lowers them in the scale of intellectual and moral beings."

It was not, however, the misuse of parental authority that created the capitalistic exploitation, whether direct or indirect, of children's labor; but, on the contrary, it was the capitalistic mode of exploitation which, by sweeping away the economical basis of parental authority, made its exercise degenerate into a mischievous misuse of power,

However terrible and disgusting the dissolution, under the capitalist system, of the old family ties may appear, nevertheless modern industry, by assigning as it does an important part in the process of production, outside the domestic sphere, to women, to young persons, and to children of both sexes, creates a new economical foundation for a higher form of the family and of the relations between the sexes. It is, of course, just as absurd to hold the Teutonic-Christian form of the family to be absolute and final as it would be to apply that character to the ancient Roman, the ancient Greek, or the Eastern forms which, moreover, taken together form a series in historic development. Moreover, it is obvious that the fact of the collective working group being composed of individuals of both sexes and all ages, must necessarily, under suitable conditions, become a source of humane development; although in its spontaneously developed, brutal, capitalistic form, where the laborer exists for the process of production, and not the process of production for the laborer, that fact is a pestiferous source of corruption and slavery.

Marx, *Capital*, Vol. I.

4. WOMEN AND CHILDREN IN THE MILLS

Let us examine somewhat more closely the fact that machinery more and more supersedes the work of men. The human labor, involved in both spinning and weaving, consists chiefly in piecing broken threads, as the machine does all the rest. This work requires no muscular strength, but only flexibility of finger. Men are, therefore, not only not needed for it, but actually, by reason of the greater muscular development of the hand, less fit for it than women and children, and are therefore naturally almost superseded by them. Hence, the more the use of the arms, the expenditure of strength, can be transferred to steam or water power, the fewer men need be employed; and as women and children work more cheaply, and in these branches better than men, they take their places.

In the spinning mills women and girls are to be found in almost exclusive possession of the throstles; among the mules one man, an adult spinner (with self-actors, he too becomes superfluous), and several piecers for tying the threads, usually children or women, sometimes young men of from eighteen to twenty years, here and there an old spinner thrown out of other employment. At the power looms women, from fifteen to twenty years, are chiefly employed, and a few men; these, however, rarely remain at this trade after their twenty-first year. Among the preparatory machinery, too, women alone are to be found, with here and there a man to clean and sharpen the carding frames. Besides all these, the factories employ numbers of children—doffers—for mounting and taking down bobbins, and a few men as overlookers, a mechanic and an engineer for the steam engines, carpenters, porters, etc., but the actual work of the mills is done by women and children. . . .

The employment of women at once breaks up the family; for when the wife spends twelve or thirteen hours every day in the mill, and the husband works the same length of time there or elsewhere, what becomes of the children? They grow up like wild weeds; they are put out to nurse for a shilling or eighteenpence a week, and how they are treated may be imagined. Hence the accidents to which little children fall victims multiply in the factory districts to a terrible extent. The lists of the Coroner of Manchester showed for nine months: 69 deaths from burning, 56 from drowning, 23 from falling, 77 from other causes, or a total of 225 deaths from accidents, while in non-manufacturing Liverpool during twelve months there were but 146 fatal accidents. The mining accidents are excluded in both cases; and, since the Coroner of Manchester has no authority in Salford, the population of both places mentioned in the comparison is about the same. The *Manchester Guardian* reports one or more deaths by burning in almost every number. That the general mortality among young children must be increased by the employment of the mothers is self-evident, and is placed beyond all doubt by notorious facts.

Women often return to the mill three or four days after confinement, leaving the baby, of course; in the dinner hour they must hurry home to feed the child and eat something, and what sort of suckling that can be is also evident.

Lord Ashley repeats the testimony of several workwomen:

"M. H., twenty years old, has two children, the youngest a baby, that is tended by the other, a little older. The mother goes to the mill shortly after five o'clock in the morning, and comes home at eight at night; all day the milk pours from her breasts so that her clothing drips with it."

"H. W. has three children, goes away Monday morning at five o'clock, and comes back Saturday evening; has so much to do for the children then that she cannot get to bed before three o'clock in the morning; often wet through to the skin, and obliged to work in that state. She said: 'My breasts have given me the most frightful pain, and I have been dripping wet with milk.' "

The use of narcotics to keep the children still is fostered by this infamous system, and has reached a great extent in the factory districts. Dr. Johns, Registrar in Chief for Manchester, is of opinion that this custom is the chief source of the many deaths from convulsions. The employment of the wife dissolves the family utterly and of necessity, and this dissolution, in our present society, which is based upon the family, brings the most demoralizing consequences for parents, as well as children. . . .

Thus the social order makes family life almost impossible for the worker. In a comfortless, filthy house, hardly good enough for mere nightly shelter, ill-furnished, often neither rain-tight nor warm, a foul atmosphere filling rooms overcrowded with human beings, no domestic comfort is possible. The husband works the whole day through, perhaps the wife also and the elder children, all in different places; they meet night and morning only, all under perpetual temptation to drink; what family life is possible under such conditions? Yet the working man cannot escape from the family, must live in the family, and the consequence is a perpetual succession of family troubles, domestic quarrels, most demoralizing for parents and children alike. Neglect of all domestic duties, neglect of the children, especially, is only too common among English working people, and only too vigorously fostered by the existing institutions of society. And children growing up in this savage way, amidst these demoralizing influences, are expected to turn out goody-goody and moral in the end! Verily the requirements are naïve which the self-satisfied bourgeois makes upon the working man!

Engels, *Condition of the Working Class in England in* 1844.

III. The Bourgeois Family

1. COMMUNISM AND THE FAMILY

Abolition of the family! Even the most radical flare up at this infamous proposal of the Communists.

On what foundation is the present family, the bourgeois family, based? On capital, on private gain. In its completely developed form this family exists only among the bourgeoisie. But this state of things finds its complement in the practical absence of the family among the proletarians, and in public prostitution.

The bourgeois family will vanish as a matter of course when its complement vanishes, and both will vanish with the vanishing of capital.

Do you charge us with wanting to stop the exploitation of children by their parents? To this crime we plead guilty.

But, you will say, we destroy the most hallowed of relations, when we replace home education by social.

And your education! Is not that also social, and determined by the social conditions under which you educate, by the intervention of society, direct or indirect, by means of schools, etc.? The Communists have not invented the intervention of society in education; they do but seek to alter the character of that intervention, and to rescue education from the influence of the ruling class.

The bourgeois claptrap about the family, and education, about the hallowed co-relation of parent and child, becomes all the more disgusting, the more, by the action of modern industry, all family ties among the proletarians are torn asunder, and their children transformed into simple articles of commerce and instruments of labor.

But you Communists would introduce community of women, screams the whole bourgeoisie in chorus.

The bourgeois sees in his wife a mere instrument of production. He hears that the instruments of production are to be exploited in common, and, naturally, can come to no other conclusion than that the lot of being common to all will likewise fall to the women.

He has not even a suspicion that the real point aimed at is to do away with the status of women as mere instruments of production.

For the rest, nothing is more ridiculous than the virtuous indignation of our bourgeois at the community of women which, they pretend, is to be openly and officially established by the Communists. The Communists have no need to introduce community of women; it has existed almost from time immemorial.

Our bourgeois, not content with having the wives and daughters of their proletarians at their disposal, not to speak of common prostitutes, take the greatest pleasure in seducing each other's wives.

Bourgeois marriage is in reality a system of wives in common and thus, at the most, what the Communists might possibly be reproached with is that they desire to introduce, in substitution for a hypocritically concealed, an openly legalized community of women. For the rest, it is self-evident, that the abolition of the present system of production must bring with it the abolition of the community of women springing from that system, *i.e.*, of prostitution both public and private.

Marx and Engels, *The Communist Manifesto.*

2. BOURGEOIS MARRIAGE

Nowadays there are two ways of concluding a bourgeois marriage. In Catholic countries the parents, as before, procure a suitable wife for their young bourgeois son, and the consequence is, of course, the fullest development of the contradiction inherent in monogamy: the husband abandons himself to hetaerism and the wife to adultery. Probably the only reason why the Catholic Church abolished divorce was because it had convinced itself that there is no more a cure for adultery than there is for death. In Protestant countries, on the other hand, the rule is that the son of bourgeois family is allowed to choose a wife from his own class with more or less freedom; hence there may be a certain element of love in the marriage, as, indeed, in accordance with Protestant hypocrisy, is always assumed for decency's sake. Here the husband's hetaerism is a more sleepy kind of business, and adultery by the wife is less the rule. But since, in every kind of marriage, people remain what they were before, and since the bourgeois of Protestant countries are mostly philistines, all that this Protestant monogamy achieves, taking the average of the best cases, is a conjugal partnership of leaden boredom, known as "domestic bliss." The best mirror of these two methods of marrying is the novel—the French novel for the Catholic manner, the German for the Protestant. In both, the hero "gets" them; in the German, the young man gets the girl; in the French, the husband gets the horns. Which of them is worse off is sometimes questionable. This is why the French bourgeois is as much horrified by the dullness of the German novel as the German philistine is by the "immorality" of the French. However, now that "Berlin is a world capital," the German novel is beginning with a little less timidity to use as part of its regular stock-in-the-trade the hetaerism and adultery long familiar to that town.

In both cases, however, the marriage is conditioned by the class position of the parties and is to that extent always a marriage of convenience. In both cases this marriage of convenience turns often enough into crassest prostitution—sometimes of both parties, but far more commonly of the woman, who only differs from the ordinary courtesan in that she does not let out her body on piece-work as a wage-worker, but sells it once and for all into slavery. And of all marriages of convenience Fourier's words hold true: "As in grammar two negatives make an affirmative, so in matrimonial morality two prostitutions pass for a virtue." Sex-love in the relationship with a woman becomes, and can only become, the real rule among the oppressed classes, which means today among the proletariat—whether this relation is officially sanctioned or not. But here all the foundations of typical monogamy are cleared away. Here there is not property, for the preservation and inheritance of which monogamy and male supremacy were established; hence there is no incentive to make this male supremacy effective. What is more, there are no means of making it so. Bourgeois law, which protects this supremacy, exist only for the possessing class and their dealings with the proletarians. The law costs money and, on account of the worker's poverty, it has no validity for his relation to his wife. Here quite other personal and social conditions decide. And now that large-scale industry has taken the wife out of the home onto the labor market and into the factory, and made her often the bread-winner of the family, no basis for any kind of male supremacy is left in the proletarian household—except, perhaps, for something of the brutality towards women that has spread since the introduction of monogamy. The proletarian family is therefore no longer monogamous in the strict sense, even where there is passionate love and firmest loyalty on both sides, and maybe all the blessings of religious and civil authority. Here, therefore, the eternal attendants of monogamy, hetaerism and adultery, play only an almost vanishing part. The wife has in fact regained the right to dissolve the marriage, and if two people cannot get on with one another, they prefer to separate. In short, proletarian marriage is monogamous in the etymological sense of the word, but not at all in its historical sense.

Our jurists, of course, find that progress in legislation is leaving women with no further ground of complaint. Modern civilized systems of law increasingly acknowledge, first, that for a marriage to be legal, it must be a contract freely entered into by both partners, and, secondly, that also in the married state both partners must stand on a common footing of equal

rights and duties. If both these demands are consistently carried out, say the jurists, women have all they can ask.

This typically legalist method of argument is exactly
the same as that which the radical republican bourgeois uses
to put the proletarian in his place. The labor contract is
to be freely entered into by both partners. But it is considered
to have ben freely entered into as soon as the law makes both
parties equal on *paper*. The power conferred on the one
party by the difference of class position, the pressure thereby
brought to bear on the other party—the real economic position of both—that is not the law's business. Again, for the
duration of the labor contract both parties are to have equal
rights, in so far as one or the other does not expressly surrender them. That economic relations compel the worker
to surrender even the last semblance of equal rights—here
again, that is no concern of the law.

In regard to marriage, the law, even the most advanced,
is fully satisfied as soon as the partners have formally recorded
that they are entering into the marriage of their own free
consent. What goes on in real life behind the juridical scenes,
how this free consent comes about—that is not the business
of the law and the jurist. And yet the most elementary comparative jurisprudence should show the jurist what this free
consent really amounts to. In the countries where an
obligatory share of the paternal inheritance is secured to the
children by law and they cannot therefore be disinherited—
in Germany, in the countries with French law and elsewhere
—the children are obliged to obtain their parents' consent to
their marriage. In the countries with English law, where
parental consent to a marriage is not legally required, the
parents on their side have full freedom in the testamentary
disposal of their property and can disinherit their children
at their pleasure. It is obvious that, in spite and precisely
because of this fact, freedom of marriage among the classes
with something to inherit is in reality not a whit greater in
England and America than it is in France and Germany.

As regards the legal equality of husband and wife in
marriage, the position is no better. The legal inequality of

the two partners, bequeathed to us from earlier social conditions, is not the cause but the effect of the economic oppression of the woman. In the old communistic household, which comprised many couples and their children, the task entrusted to the women of managing the household was as much a public and socially necessary industry as the procuring of food by the men. With the patriarchal family, and still more with the single monogamous family, a change came. Household management lost its public character. It no longer concerned society. It became a *private service;* the wife became the head servant, excluded from all participation in social production. Not until the coming of modern large-scale industry was the road to social production opened to her again—and then only to the proletarian wife. But it was opened in such a manner that, if she carries out her duties in the private service for her family, she remains excluded from public production and unable to earn; and if she wants to take part in public production and earn independently, she cannot carry out family duties. And the wife's position in the factory is the position of women in all branches of business, right up to medicine and the law. The modern individual family is founded on the open or concealed domestic slavery of the wife, and modern society is a mass composed of these individual families as its molecules.

In the great majority of cases today, at least in the possessing classes, the husband is obliged to earn a living and support his family, and that in itself gives him a position of supremacy, without any need for special legal titles and privileges. Within the family he is the bourgeois and the wife represents the proletariat. In the industrial world, the specific character of the economic oppression burdening the proletariat is visible in all its sharpness only when all special legal privileges of the capitalist .class have been abolished and complete legal equality of both classes established. The democratic republic does not do away with the opposition of the two classes; on the contrary, it provides the clear field on which the fight can be fought out. And in the same way, the peculiar character of the supremacy of the husband over the wife in the modern family, the necessity of creating real social equality between them, and the way to do it, will only be seen in the clear light of day when both possess legally complete equality of rights. Then it will be plain that the first condition for the liberation of the wife is to bring the whole female sex back into public industry, and that this in turn demands the abolition of the monogamous family as the economic unit of society.

Engels, *Origin of the Family.*

3. HOW THE BOURGEOISIE COMBATS PROSTITUTION

Recently the fifth international congress for combating the white slave traffic was held in London.

Duchesses, countesses, bishops, parsons, rabbis, police officials and all sorts of bourgeois philanthropists displayed themselves at this congress. There was no end of ceremonial banquets and sumptuous official receptions. There was no end of solemn speeches on the harm and shame of prostitution.

But what were the means of struggle which the elegant bourgeois delegates demanded at the congress? The main two means were: religion and the police. These, they said, were the surest and safest means against prostitution. According to a report by the London correspondent of the *Leipziger Volkszeitung,* an English delegate boasted of the fact that he had introduced in Parliament a bill providing for *corporal punishment* for pandering. There he is, the modern "civilized" champion of the fight against prostitution!

A certain Canadian lady expressed her enthusiasm for the police and for the women police surveillance over "fallen" women; as for raising wages, however, she remarked that working women do not deserve better pay.

A German parson fulminated against modern materialism which, he said, was spreading among the people to an ever greater extent and contributing to the spread of free love.

When the Austrian delegate Gertner ventured to mention the social causes of prostitution, the want and misery of working class families, the exploitation of child labor, the unbearable housing conditions, etc., the speaker was silenced by hostile shouts!

On the other hand, instructive and solemn stories were told among the delegates concerning various high personages. For instance, that when the German empress is about to visit a lying-in hospital in Berlin the mothers of "illegitimate" children *have rings put on their fingers,* so as to spare the high personage the shocking sight of unwedded mothers!

From this one can judge what disgusting bourgeois hypocrisy reigns at these aristocratic-bourgeois congresses. The mountebanks of charity and the police protectors of mockery at want and misery foregather to "fight against prostitution," which is maintained precisely by the aristocrats and the bourgeoisie. . . .

Lenin, *Women and Society.*

IV. Women in the Struggle for Socialism

1. THE ROLE OF WOMEN IN THE STRUGGLE FOR FREEDOM

In a certain respect this congress* of the feminine section of the proletarian army is of particularly great significance, since in all countries women have been the slowest to stir. There can be no socialist revolution, unless a vast section of the toiling women takes an important part in it.

In all civilized countries, even the most advanced, the position of women is such as justifies their being called domestic slaves. Not in a single capitalist country, not even in the freest republic, do women enjoy complete equality.

The aim of the Soviet Republic is to abolish, in the first place, all restrictions of the rights of women. The Soviet government has completely abolished the source of bourgeois filth, repression and humiliation—divorce proceedings.

For nearly a year now our completely free divorce laws have been in force. We issued a decree abolishing the difference in the status of children born in wedlock and those born out of wedlock, and also the various political disabilities. In no other country have the toiling women achieved such complete freedom and equality.

* This congress, called by the Central Committee of the Russian Communist Party, was attended by over 1,000 delegates. The congress approved the foreign policy of the Soviet government and called upon all working and peasant women to support and defend it. It also approved the proposal for drawing non-party working women into socialist construction through delegates' meetings. This congress marked the beginning of widespread work by the party among working and peasant women.—*Ed.*

We know that the entire burden of the obsolete rules is borne by the women of the working class.

Our law wiped out, for the first time in history, all that made women inferior. But it is not a matter of law. In our cities and factory settlements this law on the complete freedom of marriage is taking root, but in the countryside it very frequently exists only on paper. There, church marriage still predominates. This is due to the influence of the priests, and it is more difficult to fight this evil than the old laws.

Religious prejudices must be fought very cautiously; a lot of harm is caused by those who carry on this struggle in such a way as to offend religious feelings. The struggle must be carried on by means of propaganda, by means of enlightenment. By introducing acrimony into the struggle we may antagonize the masses; this kind of struggle contributes to the division of the masses according to religion, but our strength is in unity. The deepest source of religious prejudice is poverty and ignorance; it is with these evils that we must contend.

Up to the present the position of women has been such that it is called a position of slavery. Women are crushed by their domestic drudgery, and only socialism can relieve them from this drudgery, when we shall pass on from small household economy to social economy and to social tilling of the soil.

Only then will women be fully free and emancipated. It is a difficult task. . . .

It has been observed in the experience of all liberation movements that the success of a revolution depends on the extent to which women take part in it. The Soviet government is doing everything to enable women to carry on their proletarian socialist activity independently.

Up to the present not a single republic has been capable of emancipating the women. The Soviet government will help them. Our cause is invincible, for in all countries the invincible working class is rising. This movement signifies the growth of the invincible socialist revolution.

Lenin, *Women and Society*

2. THE GREATEST RESERVE OF THE WORKING CLASS

Not a single great movement of the oppressed in the history of mankind has been able to do without the participation of working women Working women, the most oppressed among the oppressed, never have or could stand aside from the broad path of the liberation movement. This movement of slaves has produced, as is known, hundreds and thousands of martyrs and heroines. Tens of thousands of working women were to be found in the ranks of fighters for the liberation of the serfs. It is not surprising that millions of working women have been drawn in beneath the banners of the revolutionary movement of the working class, the most powerful of all liberation movements of the oppressed masses.

International Woman's Day is a token of invincibility and an augury of the great future which lies before the liberation movement of the working class.

Working women — workers and peasants — are the greatest reserve of the working class. This reserve constitutes a good half of the population. The fate of the proletarian movement, the victory or defeat of the proletarian revolution, the victory or defeat of proletarian power depends on whether or not the reserve of women will be for or against the working class.

That is why the first task of the proletariat and its advance detachment, the Communist Party, is to engage in decisive struggle for the freeing of women workers and peasants from the influence of the bourgeoisie, for political education and the organization of women workers and peasants beneath the banner of the proletariat.

International Woman's Day is a means of winning the women's labor reserves to the side of the proletariat. Working women are not only reserves, however. They can and must become—if the working class carries out a correct policy —a real army of the working class, operating against the bourgeoisie.

The second and decisive task of the working class is to forge an army of worker and peasant women out of the women's labor reserves to operate shoulder to shoulder with the great army of the proletariat.

International Woman's Day must become a means for turning worker and peasant women from a reserve of the working class into an active army in the liberation movement of the proletariat.

Long live International Woman's Day!

Stalin: A Political Biography.

3. THE ROAD TO EMANCIPATION

The main and fundamental thing in Bolshevism and in the Russian October Revolution is the drawing into politics of precisely those who were most oppressed under capitalism. These were oppressed, deceived, and robbed by the capitalists under a monarchy as well as in democratic bourgeois republics. This oppression, this deception, this filching the toil of the people by the capitalists was inevitable as long as the private ownership of the land, the factories, and works existed.

The essence of Bolshevism, the essence of Soviet power, lies in exposing the fraud and hypocrisy of bourgeois democracy, in abolishing the private ownership of the land, the factories, and mills, and in concentrating all political power in the hands of the toilers and the exploited masses. These masses are taking politics, *i.e.*, the work of building the new society, into their own hands. This is a difficult task; the masses are downtrodden and oppressed by capitalism; but there is no other way out of wage slavery, of slavery to the capitalists, nor can there be any other way out.

And it is impossible to draw the masses into politics without also drawing in the women; for under capitalism, the female half of the human race suffers under a double yoke. The working woman and peasant woman are oppressed by capital; but in addition to that, even in the most democratic of bourgeois republics, they are, firstly, in an inferior position because the law denies them equality with men, and secondly, and this is most important, they are "in domestic slavery," they are "domestic slaves," crushed by the most petty, most menial, most arduous, and most stultifying work of the kitchen, and by isolated domestic, family economy in general.

The Bolshevik, Soviet Revolution cuts at the root of the oppression and inferiority of women more deeply than any party or any revolution in the world has dared to do. Not a trace of inequality between men and women before the law has been left in Soviet Russia. The particularly base, despicable, and hypocritical inequality of marital and family rights, inequality in relation to the child, has been completely abolished by the Soviet government.

This is only the first step towards the emancipation of women. But not a single bourgeois republic, even the most democratic, has dared to take even this first step. They dared not do so out of fear of "the sacred right of private property."

The second and principal step was the abolition of the private ownership of the land, the factories, and mills. This, and this alone, opens the way for the complete and real emancipation of women, their emancipation from "domestic slavery," by passing from petty, individual, domestic economy to large-scale social economy.

This transition is a difficult one, for it is a matter of remolding the most deep-rooted, habitual, case-hardened and ossified "system" (it would be more true to say, "outrage and barbarism," and not "system"). But the transition has been started. Things have begun to move, we have started out on the new path.

On International Working Woman's Day, in all countries in the world, at innumerable meetings of working women, greetings will be sent to Soviet Russia, which has started on unprecedently difficult and arduous, but great, universally great, and really liberating work. Encouraging appeals will be made not to lose heart in the face of the raging and often brutal bourgeois reaction. The more "free" or "democratic" the bourgeois country is, the more the capitalist gangs rave and commit their brutalities against the workers' revolution. An example of this is the democratic republic of the United States of America. But the masses of the workers have already awakened. The imperialist war has finally roused these slumbering, half-asleep, conservative masses in America, in Europe, and backward Asia.

The ice has broken in all parts of the world.

The emancipation of the peoples from the yoke of imperialism, the emancipation of the workers, men and women, from the yoke of capital, is moving irresistibly forward. This cause is being advanced by scores and hundreds of millions of working men and women and peasant men and women. That is why the emancipation of labor from the yoke of capital will be achieved the world over.

Lenin, *International Woman's Day*, 1918.

V. Socialism and the Emancipation of Women

1. THE EQUALITY OF WOMEN

Women in the U.S.S.R. are accorded equal rights with men in all spheres of economic, state, cultural, social, and political life.

The possibility of exercising these rights is ensured to women by granting them an equal right with men to work, payment for work, rest and leisure, social insurance, and education, by state protection of the interests of mother and child, by state aid to mothers of large families and unmarried mothers, pre-maternity and maternity leave with full pay, and the provision of a wide network of maternity homes, nurseries, and kindergartens.

Article 122, *Constitution of the U.S.S.R.*, 1936.

The fifth specific feature of the draft of the new Constitution is its consistent and thoroughgoing democratism. From the standpoint of democratism bourgeois constitutions may be divided into two groups: One group of constitutions openly denies, or actually nullifies, the equality of rights of citizens and democratic liberties. The other group of constitutions readily accepts, and even advertises, democratic principles, but at the same time it makes reservations and provides for restrictions which utterly mutilate these democratic rights and liberties. They speak of equal suffrage for all citizens, but at the same time limit it by residential, educational, and even property qualifications. They speak of equal rights for citizens, but at the same time they make the reservation that this does not apply to women, or that it applies to them only in part. And so on and so forth.

What distinguishes the draft of the new Constitution of the U.S.S.R. is the fact that it is free from such reservations and restrictions. For it, there exists no division of citizens into active and passive ones; for it, all citizens are active. It does not recognize any difference in rights as between men and women, "residents" and "non-residents," propertied and propertyless, educated and uneducated. For it, all citizens. have equal rights. It is not property status, not national origin, not sex, not office, but personal ability and personal labor, that determines the position of every citizen in society,

Stalin, *Selected Writings.*

2. THE TASKS OF THE WORKING WOMEN'S MOVEMENT IN THE SOVIET REPUBLIC

I should like to say a few words about the general tasks of the working women's movement in the Soviet Republic; the tasks connected with the transition to socialism in general, as well as those which are so persistently forcing their way to the forefront at the present time. Comrades, the question of the position of women was raised by the Soviet government from the very outset. In my opinion, the task of every workers' state that is passing to socialism will be of a two-fold character. The first part of this task is comparatively simple and easy. It concerns the old laws which placed women in an inferior position as compared with men.

The representatives of all liberation movements in Western Europe not only for decades but for centuries demanded the abolition of these obsolete laws and the establishment of legal equality between men and women. But not a single European democratic state, not one of the most advanced republics, has succeeded in achieving this, because where capitalism exists, where the private ownership of the land, the private ownership of factories and works is preserved, where the power of capital is preserved, men will retain their privileges. We succeeded in achieving this in Russia only because on November 7, 1917, the power of the workers was established in this country. From the very outset the Soviet government set itself the aim of existing as the government of the toilers opposed to all exploitation. It set itself the aim of destroying the possibility of landlords and capitalists exploiting the toilers, of destroying the rule of capital. The aim of the Soviet government was to create the conditions in which the toilers could build their own lives without the private ownership of the land, without the private ownership of the factories and works, without that private ownership which everywhere, all over the world, even where complete political liberty reigns, even in the most democratic republics, has actually placed the toilers in conditions of poverty and wage slavery, and women in a position of double slavery.

The Soviet government, as the government of the toilers during the very first months of its existence, brought about a complete revolution in the laws affecting women. Of the laws which placed women in a subordinate position not a trace has been left in the Soviet Republic. I speak precisely of those laws which particularly took advantage of woman's weaker position and put her in an inferior and often even in a degrading position; I refer to the divorce laws, the laws concerning children born out of wedlock, the right of a woman to sue the father of her child for maintenance.

It is precisely in this sphere that in bourgeois law, it must be said, even in the most advanced countries, advantage is taken of woman's weaker position to make her inferior and to degrade her; and it is precisely in this sphere that the Soviet government has destroyed every trace of the old unjust laws, which were intolerable for the representatives of the toiling masses. And we can now proudly say without the slightest exaggeration that except for Soviet Russia there is not a single country in the world in which there is complete equality between men and women and in which women are not placed in a degraded position, which is particularly felt in everyday family life. This was one of our first and most important tasks.

If you happen to come in contact with parties which are hostile to the Bolsheviks, or if Russian newspapers published in the regions occupied by Kolchak or Denikin happen to fall into your hands, or if you happen to speak with people who share the views of these newspapers, you will often hear accusations to the effect that the Soviet government has violated democracy.

We, the representatives of the Soviet government, the Bolshevik Communists and adherents of Soviet government, are constantly being accused of having violated democracy, and the evidence advanced to prove this is that the Soviet government dispersed the Constituent Assembly. Our usual reply to these charges is: We have no use for the kind of democracy and Constituent Assembly which arose under the system of private ownership of land, when people were not equal, when those who owned capital were the masters and the rest worked for them, were their wage slaves. This kind of democracy has served as a screen to conceal slavery even in the most advanced states. We socialists are adherents of democracy only to the extent that it alleviates the position of the toilers and oppressed. All over the world socialism pursues the aim of fighting against all exploitation of man by man. We attach real significance to the democracy which serves the exploited, those who are placed in a position of inferiority. If non-toilers are deprived of the franchise, that is real equality. He who does not work shall not eat. In reply to these accusations we say that the question that should be put is: How is democracy carried out in this or that state? We see that equality is proclaimed in all democratic republics: but in civil law, and in the laws governing the position of woman, her position in the family and in regard to divorce, we see inequality and the degradation of women at every step. And we say: This is violation of democracy, and precisely in regard to the oppressed. The Soviet government has applied democracy to a greater extent than any other country, even the most advanced, by the fact that in its laws not the slightest hint of any inferiority of women is left. I repeat, not a single state and no democratic legislation has done even half of what the Soviet government did for women in the very first months of its existence.

Of course, laws are not enough, and we cannot under any circumstances be satisfied merely with what we say in our laws; but we have done all that was expected of us to make women equal with men, and we have a right to be proud of what we have done. The position of women in Soviet Russia is now an ideal position from the point of view of the most advanced states. But we say to ourselves: Of course this is only a beginning.

As long as women are engaged in housework their position is still a restricted one. In order to achieve the complete emancipation of women and to make them really equal with men, we must have social economy, and the participation of women in general productive labor. Then women will occupy the same position as men.

This, of course, does not mean that women must be exactly equal with men in productivity of labor, amount of labor, its duration, conditions of labor, etc. But it does mean that women shall not be in an oppressed economic position compared with men. You all know that even with the fullest equality, women are still in an actual position of inferiority because all housework is thrust upon them. Most of this housework is highly unproductive, most barbarous and most arduous, and it is performed by women. This labor is extremely petty and contains nothing that would in the slightest degree facilitate the development of women.

In pursuit of our socialist ideals we want to fight for the complete realization of socialism, and here a wide field of work is opened up for women. We are now seriously preparing to clear the ground for socialist construction; and the construction of socialist society will commence only when we, having achieved the complete equality of women, take up our new work together with women who have been emancipated from petty, stultifying, unproductive work. This work is sufficient to last us for many, many years. This work cannot produce such quick results and will not create such a striking effect.

We are establishing model institutions, dining rooms and *crèches,* which will liberate women from housework. And it is precisely the women primarily who must undertake the work of building all these institutions. It must be said that at present there are very few such institutions in Russia that could help the women to liberate themselves from their state of domestic slavery. The number is insignificant, and the conditions in which the Soviet Republic is now placed—the military and food conditions about which the other comrades have spoken to you at length—hinder us in this work. Nevertheless, it must be said that such institutions, which liberate women from their position of domestic slavery, are springing up wherever there is the slightest possibility for them to do so. We say that the emancipation of the workers must be brought about by the workers themselves, and similarly, the emancipation of women workers must be brought about by the women workers themselves. Women workers themselves should see to the development of such institutions; and their activities in this field will lead to a complete change from the position they formerly occupied in capitalist society.

In order to engage in politics in the old capitalist society, special training was required; that is why women's participation in politics, even in the most advanced and free capitalist countries, is insignificant. Our task is to make politics accessible to every toiling woman. From the moment the private ownership of land and factories was abolished and the power of the landlords and capitalists was overthrown, the tasks of politics became simple, clear, and quite accessible to all the toiling masses, and to the toiling women. In capitalist society women are placed in such an inferior position that their participation in politics is insignificant compared with that of men. In order to change this state of affairs the rule of the toilers is required, and when that is achieved the principal tasks of politics will consist of all that which directly concerns the fate of the toilers themselves.

And here the participation of the women workers, not only of party and class conscious women workers, but also of non-party and the least class conscious, is necessary. In this respect, the Soviet government opens up a wide field of activity for women workers.

We have experienced very hard times in the struggle against the forces hostile to Soviet Russia which are marching against us. It has been very hard for us to fight in the military field against these forces which are waging war against the rule of the toilers, and in the food field against the profiteers, because the number of people, of toilers, who come forward wholeheartedly to help us by their labor, is not yet sufficiently large. And so the Soviet government prizes nothing so highly as the assistance of the broad masses of non-party working women. Let them know that perhaps in the old bourgeois society a complicated training was required in order to engage in political activity, and that this was inaccessible to women. But the principal aim of political activity in the Soviet Republic is to fight against the landlords and the capitalists, to fight for the abolition of exploitation; and this opens for the women workers in the Soviet Republic a field for political activity which will consist of utilizing their organizing ability to help the men.

We not only need organizational work on a scale affecting millions, we also need organizational work on the smallest scale that women will also be able to engage in. Women can work amidst war conditions as well, when it is a matter of helping the army, of carrying on agitation in its ranks. Women must take an active part in this, so that the Red Army may see that it is being cared for and looked after. Women may also work in the food field, in distributing food, in improving the work of catering for the masses, in setting up more dining rooms, such as have now been opened on so wide a scale in Petrograd.

It is in these fields that the activity of the working women acquires real organizational significance. The participation of women is also required in the organization of large experimental enterprises and in supervising them so that this shall not be the work of isolated individuals. Without the participation of a large number of toiling women in this work, it cannot be accomplished. And working women are quite competent in this field for such work as supervising the distribution of food and seeing that provisions are more easily obtained. This is work that non-party working women can easily do, and at the same time it is work that will help most of all firmly to establish socialist society.

Having abolished the private ownership of land and having almost entirely abolished the private ownership of factories and works, the Soviet government strives to enlist all toilers, not only party, but also non-party, not only men, but also women, in the work of economic construction. This work begun by the Soviet government can be advanced only when, instead of hundreds of women, we have millions and millions of women, all over Russia, taking part in it. When that is the case, we are convinced, the work of socialist construction will be firmly established. Then the toilers will show that they can live and administer without landlords and capitalists. Then socialist construction will be so firmly established in Russia that the Soviet Republic will have no cause to fear any external enemies in other countries, or enemies within Russia.

Lenin, *Women and Society.*

3. AGAINST HOUSEHOLD DRUDGERY

. . . Take the position of women. Not a single democratic party in the world, not even in any of the most advanced bourgeois republics, has done in this sphere in tens of years a hundredth part of what we did in the very first year we were in power. In the literal sense, we did not leave a single brick standing of the despicable laws which placed women in a state of inferiority compared with men, of the laws restricting divorce, of the disgusting formalities attending divorce proceedings, of the laws on illegitimate children and on searching for their fathers, etc. To the shame of the bourgeoisie and of capitalism, be it said, numerous survivals of these laws exist in all civilized countries. We have the right a thousand times to be proud of what we have done in this sphere. But the more *thoroughly* we have cleared the ground of the lumber of the old, bourgeois, laws and institutions, the more apparent has it become to us that we have only cleared the ground for the structure; the structure itself has not been built as yet.

Notwithstanding all the liberating laws that have been passed, woman continues to be a *domestic slave,* because *petty housework* crushes, strangles, stultifies and degrades her, chains her to the kitchen and to the nursery, and wastes her labor on barbarously unproductive, petty, nerve-racking, stultifying and crushing drudgery. The real *emancipation of women,* real communism, will begin only when a mass struggle (led by the proletariat which is in power) is started against this petty domestic economy, or rather when it is *transformed on a mass scale* into large-scale socialist economy.

Do we in practice devote sufficient attention to this question, which, theoretically, is indisputable for every Communist? Of course not. Do we devote sufficient care to the *young shoots* of communism which have already sprung up in this sphere? Again we must say emphatically, No! Public dining rooms, *crèches,* kindergartens—these are examples of the shoots, the simple everyday means, which assume nothing pompous, grandiloquent or solemn, but which can *in fact emancipate women,* which can in fact lessen and abolish their inferiority to men in regard to their role in social production and in social life. These means are not new, they (like all the material prerequisites for socialism) were created by large-scale capitalism; but under capitalism they remained, first, a rarity, and, second, and what is particularly important, either *profit-making* enterprises, with all the worst features of speculation, profiteering, cheating and fraud, or the "acrobatics of bourgeois philanthropy," which the best workers quite rightly hated and despised.

There is no doubt that the number of these institutions in our country has greatly increased and that they are *begin-*

ning to change in character. There is no doubt that there is far more *organizing* talent among the working women and peasant women than we are aware of, people who are able to organize in a practical way and enlist large numbers of workers, and a still larger number of consumers, for this purpose without the abundance of phrases, fuss, squabbling and chatter about plans, systems, etc., which our swelled-headed "intelligentsia" or half-baked "Communists" always suffer from. But we do not *nurse* these new shoots with sufficient care.

Look at the bourgeoisie! How well it is able to advertise what *it* requires! See how what the capitalists regard as "model" enterprises are praised in millions of copies of *their* newspapers; see how "model" bourgeois enterprises are transformed into objects of national pride! Our press does not take the trouble, or hardly takes the trouble, to describe the best dining rooms or *crèches*, to secure by daily exhortation the transformation of some of them into models. It does not give them enough publicity, does not describe in detail what saving in human labor, what conveniences for the consumer, what a saving in products, what emancipation of women from domestic slavery and what an improvement in sanitary conditions can be achieved with *exemplary Communist labor* for the whole of society, for all the toilers.

Lenin, *Women and Society.*

4. FREEDOM AND EQUALITY

The second anniversary of the Soviet power is a fitting occasion for us to review what has, in general, been accomplished during this period, and to probe into the significance and aims of the revolution which we accomplished.

The bourgeoisie and its supporters accuse us of violating democracy. We maintain that the Soviet revolution has given an unprecedented stimulus to the development of democracy both in depth and breadth, of democracy, moreover, distinctly for the toiling masses, which had been oppressed under capitalism; consequently, of democracy for the vast majority of the people, of socialist democracy (for the toilers) as distinguished from bourgeois democracy (for the exploiters, the capitalists, the rich).

Who is right?

To probe deeply into this question and to understand it well will mean studying the experience of these two years and being better prepared to further follow up this experience.

The position of women furnishes a particularly graphic elucidation of the difference between bourgeois and socialist democracy, it furnishes a particularly graphic answer to the posed question.

In no bourgeois republic (*i.e.,* where there is private ownership of the land, factories, works, shares, etc.), be it even the most democratic republic, *nowhere in the world, not even in the most advanced country,* have women gained a position of complete equality. And this, notwithstanding the fact that more than one and a quarter centuries have elapsed since the Great French (bourgeois-democratic) Revolution.

In words, bourgeois democracy promises equality and liberty. In fact, *not* a single bourgeois republic, not even the most advanced one, *has given* the feminine half of the human race either full legal equality with men or freedom from the guardianship and oppression of men.

Bourgeois democracy is democracy of pompous phrases, solemn words, exuberant promises, and the high-sounding slogans of *freedom and equality*. But, in fact, it screens the non-freedom and inferiority of women, the non-freedom and inferiority of the toilers and exploited.

Soviet, or socialist, democracy sweeps aside the pompous, but lying, words, declares ruthless war on the hypocrisy of the "democrats," the landlords, capitalists or well-fed peasants who are making money by selling their surplus bread to hungry workers at profiteering prices.

Down with this contemptible fraud! There cannot be, nor is there or will there ever be "equality" between the oppressed and the oppressors, between the exploited and the exploiters. There cannot be, nor is there or will there ever be real "freedom" as long as there is no freedom for women from the privileges which the law grants to men, as long as there is no freedom from the workers from the yoke of capital, and no freedom for the toiling peasants from the yoke of the capitalists, landlords and merchants.

Let the liars and hypocrites, the dull-witted and blind, the bourgeois and their supporters hoodwink the people with talk about freedom in general, about equality in general, about democracy in general.

We say to the workers and peasants: Tear the masks from the faces of these liars, open the eyes of these blind ones. Ask them:

"Equality between what sex and what other sex?

"Between what nation and what other nation?

"Between what class and what other class?

"Freedom from what yoke, or from the yoke of what class? Freedom for what class?"

Whoever speaks of politics, of democracy, of liberty, of equality, of socialism, and does not at the same time *ask* these questions, does not put them in the foreground, does not fight against concealing, hushing up and glossing over these questions, is of the worst enemies of the toilers, is a wolf in sheep's clothing, is a bitter opponent of the workers and peasants, is a servant of the landlords, tsars, capitalists.

In the course of two years Soviet power in one of the most backward countries of Europe did more to emancipate women and to make their status equal to that of the "strong" sex than all the advanced, enlightened, "democratic" republics of the world did in the course of a hundred and thirty years.

Enlightenment, culture, civilization, liberty—in all capitalist, bourgeois republics of the world all these fine words are combined with extremely infamous, disgustingly filthy and brutally coarse laws in which woman is treated as an inferior being, laws dealing with marriage rights and divorce, with the inferior status of a child born out of wedlock as compared with that of a "legitimate" child, laws granting privileges to men, laws that are humiliating and insulting to women.

The yoke of capital, the tyranny of "sacred private property," the despotism of philistine stupidity, the greed of petty proprietors—these are the things that prevented the most democratic bourgeois republics from infringing upon those filthy and infamous laws.

The Soviet Republic, the republic of workers and peasants, promptly wiped out these laws and left not a stone in the structure of bourgeois fraud and bourgeois hypocrisy.

Down with this fraud! Down with the liars who are talking of freedom and equality *for all*, while there is an oppressed sex, while there are oppressor classes, while there is private ownership of capital, of shares, while there are the well-fed with their surplus of bread who keep the hungry in bondage. Not freedom for all, not equality for all, but a *fight* against the oppressors and exploiters, the *abolition of every possibility* of oppression and exploitation—that is our slogan!

Freedom and equality for the oppressed sex!

Freedom and equality for the workers, for the toiling peasants!

A fight against the oppressors, a fight against the capitalists, a fight against the profiteering kulaks!

That is our fighting slogan, that is our proletarian truth, the truth of the struggle against capital, the truth which we flung in the face of the world of capital with its honeyed, hypocritical, pompous phrases about freedom and equality *in general*, about freedom and equality *for all*.

And for the very reason that we have torn down the mask of this hypocrisy, that we are introducing with revolutionary energy freedom and equality for the oppressed and for the toilers, against the oppressors, against the capitalists, against the kulaks—for this very reason the Soviet government has become so dear to the hearts of workers of the whole world.

It is for this very reason that, on the second anniversary of the Soviet power, the sympathies of the masses of the workers, the sympathies of the oppressed and exploited in every country of the world, are with us.

It is for this very reason that, on this second anniversary of the Soviet power, despite hunger and cold, despite all our tribulations, which have been caused by the imperialists' invasion of the Russian Soviet Republic, we are full of firm faith in the justice of our cause, of firm faith in the inevitable victory of Soviet power all over the world.

Lenin, *Women and Society.*

5. ELECT MORE WOMEN WORKERS!

The elections to the Moscow Soviet show that the party of the Communists is gaining strength among the working class.

It is essential that women workers take a greater part in the elections. The Soviet government was the first and only government in the world that abolished completely all the old, bourgeois, infamous laws which placed women in an inferior position compared with men and which granted privileges to men, as, for instance, in the sphere of marriage laws or in the sphere of the legal attitude to children. The Soviet government was the first and only government in the world which, as a government of the toilers, abolished all the privileges connected with property, which men retained in the family laws of all bourgeois republics, even the most democratic.

Where there are landlords, capitalists and merchants, there can be no equality between women and men even in law.

Where there are no landlords, capitalists and merchants, where the government of the toilers is building a new life without these exploiters, there equality between women and men exists in law.

But that is not enough.

It is a far cry from equality in law to equality in life.

We want women workers to achieve equality with men workers not only in law, but in life as well. For this, it is essential that women workers take an ever increasing part in the administration of public enterprises and in the administration of the state.

By engaging in the work of administration women will learn quickly and they will catch up with the men.

Therefore, elect more women workers, both Communist and non-party, to the Soviet. If one is only an honest woman worker who is capable of managing work sensibly and conscientiously, it makes no difference if she is not a member of the party—elect her to the Moscow Soviet.

Let there be more women workers in the Moscow Soviet! Let the Moscow proletariat show that it is prepared to do and is doing everything for the fight to victory, for the fight against the old inequality, against the old, bourgeois humiliation of women!

The proletariat cannot achieve complete freedom, unless it achieves complete freedom for women.

Lenin, *Women and Society*.

6. REAL, NOT FORMAL, EQUALITY

Capitalism combines formal equality with economic and, consequently, social inequality. This is one of the principal distinguishing features of capitalism, one that is mendaciously screened by the supporters of the bourgeoisie, the liberals, and that is not understood by the petty-bourgeois democrats. Out of this distinguishing feature of capitalism, by the way, the necessity arises, while fighting resolutely for economic equality, openly to recognize capitalist inequality and, under certain conditions, even to include this open recognition of inequality as a basis for the proletarian state organization (the Soviet constitution).

But capitalism *cannot* be consistent even with regard to formal equality (equality before the law, "equality" between the well-fed and the hungry, between the property-owner and the propertyless). And one of the most flagrant manifestations of this inconsistency is the *inferior position* of woman compared with man. Not a single bourgeois state, not even the most progressive, republican democratic state, has brought about complete equality of rights.

But the Soviet Republic of Russia promptly wiped out, *without any exception,* every trace of inequality in the legal status of woman, and secured her complete equality in its laws.

It is said that the level of culture is best characterized by the legal status of woman. There is a grain of profound truth in this saying. From this point of view, only the dictatorship of the proletariat, only the socialist state, could achieve and did achieve a higher level of culture.

Therefore, the foundation (and consolidation) of the first Soviet Republic—and alongside and in connection with this, the Communist International—inevitably lends a new, unparalleled, powerful impetus to the working women's movement.

For, when we speak of those who, under capitalism, were directly or indirectly, wholly or partially oppressed, it is precisely the Soviet system, and the Soviet system only, that secures democracy. This is clearly demonstrated by the position of the working class and the poor peasants. It is clearly demonstrated by the position of women.

But the Soviet system represents the final decisive conflict for the *abolition of classes,* for economic and social equality. *For us,* democracy, even democracy for those who were oppressed under capitalism, including democracy for the oppressed sex, *is inadequate.*

The working women's movement has for its object the fight for the economic and social, and not merely formal, equality of woman. The main task is to draw the women into socially productive labor, extricate them from "domestic slavery," free them of their stultifying and humiliating resignation to the perpetual and exclusive atmosphere of the kitchen and nursery.

It is a long struggle, requiring a radical remaking both of social technique and of customs. But this struggle will end with the complete triumph of communism.

Lenin, *Women and Society.*

7. THE POLITICAL EDUCATION OF WOMEN

It is five years since the Central Committee of our party convened in Moscow the All-Russian women workers' and peasants' congress. Over a thousand delegates, representing one million working women, gathered at the congress. This congress was a landmark in the work of our party among working women. The incalculable service rendered by this congress was to lay the foundation for the *organization* of the political education of our working class and peasant women.

Some may think that there is nothing out of the ordinary in this, since the party has always carried on political education among the masses, including women, or it may be thought that the political education of women can have no real importance since we shall soon have united worker and peasant cadres. Such opinions are fundamentally incorrect.

The political education of working women is of primary importance today when power has passed into the hands of the workers and peasants. Let me explain why.

Our country has a population of nearly 140 million and no less than half are women, mainly working class and peasant women, backward, downtrodden, and with little political consciousness.

If our country has begun the construction of the new Soviet life in earnest, then surely it is clear that the women of this country, constituting half its population, would act as a drag on any advance if they remained backward, downtrodden, and politically undeveloped in the future also?

The woman worker stands shoulder to shoulder with the man worker. She works with him in the common task of building our industry. She can help the common cause if she is politically conscious and politically educated. But she can ruin the common cause if she is downtrodden and backward, not, of course, as a result of her ill-will, but because of her backwardness.

The peasant woman stands shoulder to shoulder with the peasant man. She advances, together with him, the common cause of the development of our agriculture, its successes, and its flourishing.

She can make an enormous contribution in this cause if she frees herself of backwardness and ignorance. And the contrary is also the case: she could act as a brake on the whole cause if she remains a slave to ignorance in the future also.

Working class and peasant women are free citizens on an equal footing with working class and peasant men. The women elect our Soviets and our co-operatives and can be elected to these organs. Working class and peasant women, if they are politically literate, can improve our Soviets and co-operatives, strengthen and develop them. Working class and peasant women, if they are backward and ignorant, can weaken and undermine these organizations.

Finally, working class and peasant women are mothers who bring up our youth—the future of our country. They can cripple the spirit of a child or give us youth with a healthy spirit, capable of taking our country forward. All this depends on whether the woman and mother has sympathy for the Soviet system or whether she trails in the wake of the priest, the kulak, or the bourgeois.

That is why the political education of working class and peasant women is a task of primary importance, a most important task for real victory over the bourgeoisie today, when the workers and peasants have set about the building of a new life. That is why the importance of the first working class and peasant women's congress, which laid the foundations for the task of politically educating working women, is really quite inestimable.

Five years ago at that congress, the current task of the party was to draw hundreds of thousands of *working women* into the common task of building a new Soviet life. In the forefront of this task there stood women workers from the industrial areas, since they were the most lively and conscious elements among working women. It may be said that a good deal has been done in this respect in the past five years although much still remains to be done.

Today, the party's current task is to draw millions of *peas-*

ant women into the common cause of organizing our Soviet life.

Five years of work have already produced a whole number of leading personnel who have emerged from among the peasantry.

Let us hope that the ranks of the leading women peasants will be swelled by the addition of fresh, politically conscious, peasant women. Let us hope that the party will solve this problem also.

Stalin, *Collected Works.*

VI. The Relation of Sexes

1. THE FUTURE OF MARRIAGE

We thus have three principal forms of marriage which correspond broadly to the three principal stages of human development. For the period of savagery, group marriage; for barbarism, pairing marriage; for civilization, monogamy, supplemented by adultery and prostitution. Between pairing marriage and monogamy intervenes a period in the upper stage of barbarism when men have female slaves at their command and polygamy is practiced.

As our whole presentation has shown, the progress which manifests itself in these successive forms is connected with the peculiarity that women, but not men, are increasingly deprived of the sexual freedom of group marriage. In fact, for men group marriage actually still exists even to this day. What for the woman is a crime, entailing grave legal and social consequences, is considered honorable in a man or, at the worse, a slight moral blemish which he cheerfully bears. But the more the hetaerism of the past is changed in our time by capitalist commodity production and brought into conformity with it, the more, that is to say, it is transformed into undisguised prostitution, the more demoralizing are its effects. And it demoralizes men far more than women. Among women, prostitution degrades only the unfortunate ones who become its victims, and even these by no means to the extent commonly believed. But it degrades the character of the whole male world. A long engagement, particularly, is in nine cases out of ten a regular preparatory school for conjugal infidelity.

We are now approaching a social revolution in which the economic foundations of monogamy as they have existed hitherto will disappear just as surely as those of its complement—prostitution. Monogamy arose from the concentration of considerable wealth in the hands of a single individual—a man—and from the need to bequeath this wealth to the children of that man and of no other. For this purpose, the monogamy of the woman was required, not that of the man, so this monogamy of the woman did not in any way interfere with open or concealed polygamy on the part of the man. But by transforming by far the greater portion, at any rate, of permanent, heritable wealth—the means of production—into social property, the coming social revolution will reduce to a minimum all this anxiety about bequeathing and inheriting. Having arisen from economic causes, will monogamy then disappear when these causes disappear?

One might answer, not without reason: far from disappearing, it will, on the contrary, be realized completely. For with the transformation of the means of production into social property there will disappear also wage-labor, the proletariat, and therefore the necessity for a certain—statistically calculable—number of women to surrender themselves for money. Prostitution disappears; monogamy, instead of collapsing, at last becomes a reality—also for men.

In any case, therefore, the position of men will be very much altered. But the position of women, of *all* women, also undergoes significant change. With the transfer of the means of production into common ownership, the single family ceases to be the economic unit of society. Private housekeeping is transformed into a social industry. The care and education of the children becomes a public affair; society looks after all children alike, whether they are legitimate or not. This removes all the anxiety about the "consequences," which today is the most essential social—moral as well as economic —factor that prevents a girl from giving herself completely to the man she loves. Will not that suffice to bring about the gradual growth of unconstrained sexual intercourse and with it a more tolerant public opinion in regard to a maiden's

honor and a woman's shame? And, finally, have we not seen
that in the modern world monogamy and prostitution are
indeed contradictions, but inseparable contradictions, poles
of the same state of society? Can prostitution disappear without dragging monogamy with it into the abyss?

Here a new element comes into play, an element which,
at the time when monogamy was developing, existed at most
in germ: individual sex-love.

Before the Middle Ages we cannot speak of individual sex-
love. That personal beauty, close intimacy, similarity of tastes,
and so forth awakened in people of opposite sex the desire
for sexual intercourse, that men and women were not totally
indifferent regarding the partner with whom they entered
into this most intimate relationship—that goes without saying. But it is still a very long way to our sexual love. Throughout the whole of antiquity, marriages were arranged by the
parents, and the partners calmly accepted their choice. What
little love there was between husband and wife in antiquity
is not so much subjective inclination as objective duty, not
the cause of the marriage, but its corollary. Love relationships
in the modern sense only occur in antiquity outside official
society. The shepherds of whose joys and sorrows in love
Theocritus and Moschus sing, the Daphnis and Chloe of
Longus are all slaves who have no part in the state, the free
citizen's sphere of life. Except among slaves, we find love
affairs only as products of the disintegration of the old world
and carried on with women who also stand outside official
society, with *hetairai*—that is, with foreigners or freed slaves:
in Athens from the eve of its decline, in Rome under the
Caesars. If there were any real love affairs between free men
and free women, these occurred only in the course of adultery.
And to the classical love poet of antiquity, old Anacreon,
sexual love in our sense mattered so little that it did not even
matter to him which sex his beloved was.

Our sexual love differs essentially from the simple sexual
desire, the Eros, of the ancients. In the first place, it assumes
that the person loved returns the love; to this extent the
woman is on an equal footing with the man, whereas in the

Eros of antiquity she was often not even asked. Secondly, our sexual love has a degree of intensity and duration which makes both lovers feel that non-possession and separation are a great, if not the greatest, calamity; to possess one another, they risk high stakes, even life itself. In the ancient world this happened only, if at all, in adultery. And, finally, there arises a new moral standard in the judgment of a sexual relationship. We do not only ask, was it within or outside marriage? but also, did it spring from love and reciprocated love or not? Of course, this new standard has fared no better in feudal or bourgeois practice than all the other standards of morality—it is ignored. But neither does it fare any worse. It is recognized just as much as they are—in theory, on paper. And for the present it cannot ask anything more.

At the point where antiquity broke off its advance to sexual love, the Middle Ages took it up again: in adultery. We have already described the knightly love which gave rise to the songs of dawn. From the love which strives to break up marriage to the love which is to be its foundation there is still a long road, which chivalry never fully traversed. Even when we pass from the frivolous Latins to the virtuous Germans, we find in the *Nibelungenlied* that, although in her heart Kriemhild is as much in love with Siegfried as he is with her, yet when Gunther announces that he has promised her to a knight he does not name, she simply replies: "You have no need to ask me; as you bid me, so will I ever be; whom you, lord, give me as husband, him will I gladly take in troth." It never enters her head that her love can be even considered. Gunther asks for Brünhild in marriage, and Etzel for Kriemhild, though they have never seen them. Similarly, in *Gutrun,* Sigebant of Ireland asks for the Norwegian Ute, whom he has never seen, Hetel of Hegelingen for Hilde of Ireland, and, finally, Siegfried of Moorland, Hartmut of Ormany and Herwig of Seeland for Gutrun, and here Gutrun's acceptance of Herwig is for the first time voluntary. As a rule, the young prince's bride is selected by his parents, if they are still living, or, if not, by the prince himself, with the advice of the great feudal lords, who have a weighty word to say in all these cases. Nor can it be otherwise. For the knight or baron, as for the prince of the land himself, marriage is a political act, an opportunity to increase power by new alliances; the interest of the *house* must be decisive, not the wishes of an individual. What chance then is there for love to have the final word in the making of a marriage?

The same thing holds for the guild member in the medieval towns. The very privileges protecting him, the guild charters with all their clauses and rubrics, the intricate distinctions legally separating him from other guilds, from the members of his own guild or from his journeymen and apprentices, already made the circle narrow enough within which he could look for a suitable wife. And who in the circle was the most suitable was decided under this complicated system most certainly not by his individual preference but by the family interests.

In the vast majority of cases, therefore, marriage remained, up to the close of the Middle Ages, what it had been from the start—a matter which was not decided by the partners. In the beginning, people were already born married—married to an entire group of the opposite sex. In the later forms of group marriage similar relations probably existed, but with the group continually contracting. In the pairing marriage it was customary for the mothers to settle the marriages of their children; here, too, the decisive considerations are the new ties of kinship, which are to give the young pair a stronger position in the gens and tribe. And when, with the preponderance of private over communal property and the interest in its bequeathal, father-right and monogamy gained supremacy, the dependence of marriages on economic considerations became complete. The *form* of marriage by purchase disappears, the actual practice is steadily extended until not only the woman but also the man acquires a price—not according to his personal qualities, but according to his property. That the mutual affection of the people concerned should be the one paramount reason for marriage, outweighing everything else, was and always had been absolutely unheard of in the practice of the ruling classes; that sort of thing only happened in romance—or among the oppressed classes, who did not count.

Such was the state of things encountered by capitalist production when it began to prepare itself, after the epoch of geographical discoveries, to win world power by world trade and manufacture. One would suppose that this manner of marriage exactly suited it, and so it did. And yet—there are no limits to the irony of history—capitalist production itself was to make the decisive breach in it. By changing all things into commodities, it dissolved all inherited and traditional relationships, and, in place of time-honored custom and historic right, it set up purchase and sale, "free" contract. And the English jurist, H. S. Maine, thought he had made a tremendous discovery when he said that our whole progress in comparison with former epochs consisted in the fact that we had passed "from status to contract," from inherited to freely contracted conditions—which, in so far as it is correct, was already in *The Communist Manifesto* [Chapter II].

But a contract requires people who can dispose freely of their persons, actions, and possessions, and meet each other on the footing of equal rights. To create these "free" and "equal" people was one of the main tasks of capitalist production. Even though at the start it was carried out only half-consciously, and under a religious disguise at that, from the time of the Lutheran and Calvinist Reformation the principle was established that man is only fully responsible for his actions when he acts with complete freedom of will, and that it is a moral duty to resist all coercion to an immoral act. But how did this fit in with the hitherto existing practice in the arrangement of marriages? Marriage, according to the bourgeois conception, was a contract, a legal transaction, and the most important one of all, because it disposed of two human beings, body and mind, for life. Formally, it is true, the contract at that time was entered into voluntarily: without the assent of the persons concerned, nothing could be done. But everyone knew only too well how this assent was obtained and who were the real contracting parties in the marriage. But if real freedom of decision was required for all other contracts, then why not for this? Had not the two young people to be coupled also the right to dispose freely of themselves, of their bodies and organs? Had not chivalry brought sex-love into fashion, and was not its proper bourgeois form, in contrast to chivalry's adulterous love, the love of husband and wife? And if it was the duty of married people to love each other, was it not equally the duty of lovers to marry each other and nobody else? Did not this right of the lovers stand higher than the right of parents, relations, and other traditional marriage-brokers and matchmakers? If the right of free, personal discrimination broke boldly into the Church and religion, how should it halt before the intolerable claim of the older generation to dispose of the body, soul, property, happiness, and unhappiness of the younger generation?

These questions inevitably arose at a time which was loosening all the old ties of society and undermining all traditional conceptions. The world had suddenly grown almost ten times bigger; instead of one quadrant of a hemisphere, the whole globe lay before the gaze of the West Europeans, who hastened to take the other seven quadrants into their possession. And with the old narrow barriers of their homeland fell also the thousand-year-old barriers of the prescribed medieval way of thought. To the outward and the inward eye of man opened an infinitely wider horizon. What did a young man care about the approval of respectability, or honorable guild privileges handed down for generations, when the wealth of India beckoned to him, the gold and the silver mines of Mexico and Potosi? For the bourgeoisie, it was the time of knight-errantry; they, too, had their romance and their raptures of love, but on a bourgeois footing and, in the last analysis, with bourgeois aims.

So it came about that the rising bourgeoisie, especially in Protestant countries, where existing conditions had been most severely shaken, increasingly recognized freedom of contract also in marriage, and carried it into effect in the manner described. Marriage remained class marriage, but within the class the partners were conceded a certain degree of freedom of choice. And on paper, in ethical theory and in poetic description, nothing was more immutably established than that every marriage is immoral which does not rest on mutual sexual love and really free agreement of husband and wife. In short, the love marriage was proclaimed as a human right, and indeed not only as a *droit de l'homme,* one of the rights of man, but also, for once in a way, as *droit de la femme,* one of the rights of woman.

This human right, however, differed in one respect from all other so-called human rights. While the latter, in practice, remain restricted to the ruling class (the bourgeoisie), and are directly or indirectly curtailed for the oppressed class (the proletariat), in the case of the former the irony of history plays another of its tricks. The ruling class remains dominated by the familiar economic influences and therefore only in exceptional cases does it provide instances of really freely contracted marriages, while among the oppressed class, as we have seen, these marriages are the rule.

Full freedom of marriage can therefore only be generally established when the abolition of capitalist production and of the property relations created by it has removed all the accompanying economic considerations which still exert such a powerful influence on the choice of a marriage partner. For then there is no other motive left except mutual inclination.

And as sexual love is by its nature exclusive—although at present this exclusiveness is fully realized only in the woman—the marriage based on sexual love is by its nature individual marriage. We have seen how right Bachofen was in regarding the advance from group marriage to individual marriage as primarily due to the women. Only the step from pairing marriage to monogamy can be put down to the credit of the men, and historically the essence of this was to make the position of the women worse and the infidelities of the men easier. If now the economic considerations also disappear which made women put up with the habitual infidelity of their husbands—concern for their own means of existence and still more for their children's future—then, according to all previous experience, the equality of woman thereby achieved will tend infinitely more to make men really monogamous than to make women polyandrous.

But what will quite certainly disappear from monogamy are all the features stamped upon it through its origin in property relations; these are, in the first place, supremacy of the man, and, secondly, indissolubility. The supremacy of the man in marriage is the simple consequence of his economic supremacy, and with the abolition of the latter will disappear of itself. The indissolubility of marriage is partly a consequence of the economic situation in which monogamy arose, partly tradition from the period when the connection between this economic situation and monogamy was not yet fully understood and was carried to extremes under a religious form. Today it is already broken through at a thousand points. If only the marriage based on love is moral, then also only the marriage in which love continues. But the intense emotion of individual sex-love varies very much in duration from one individual to another, especially among men, and if affection definitely comes to an end or is supplanted by a new passionate love, separation is a benefit for both partners as well as for society—only people will then be spared having to wade through the useless mire of a divorce case.

What we can now conjecture about the way in which sexual relations will be ordered after the impending overthrow of capitalist production is mainly of a negative character, limited for the most part to what will disappear. But what will there be new? That will be answered when a new generation has grown up: a generation of men who never in their lives have known what it is to buy a woman's surrender with money or any other social instrument of power; a generation of women who have never known what it is to give themselves to a man from any other considerations than real love, or to refuse to give themselves to their lover from fear of the economic consequences. When these people are in the world, they will care precious little what anybody today thinks they ought to do; they will make their own practice and their corresponding public opinion about the practice of each individual—and that will be the end of it.

Engels, *Origin of the Family.*

2. "FREE LOVE"

Two letters to Inessa Armand

Dear friend:

I would very much advise you to be more explicit in the draft of your pamphlet; otherwise too much remains unclear.

I want to express my opinion now on one of the points you make. I suggest you entirely throw out paragraph 3 "demand (by the woman) for free love." This is indeed not a proletarian but a bourgeois demand. What do you really mean by it? What *can* one mean by it?

(1) Freedom from material (financial) calculations in love?

From:

(2) material cares?

(3) religious prejudices?

(4) paternal injunctions, etc.?

(5) the prejudices of "society"?

(6) a petty milieu (peasant, petty bourgeois, bourgeois intellectual)?

(7) the toils of the law, the courts, the police?

(8) serious problems in love?

(9) childbirth?

(10) that this makes possible adultery, etc.?

I have made a number of points (not all, of course). I don't think you mean points 8 to 10, but rather points 1 to 7, or something approximating to points 1 to 7.

For these points 1 to 7, however, you should choose some other connotation, since the term "free love" does not exactly express these concepts.

The public and the readers of the pamphlet will *inevitably* understand something like points 8 to 10, even if *that was not your intention:* Because the noisiest and most talkative classes in contemporary society, those of the "social set," understand by free love points 8 to 10, your demand is bourgeois, not proletarian.

For the proletariat the most important points are, firstly, 1 and 2, and then 1 to 7, but these do not really embody the term "free love."

The question is not what "you would like to understand" by this *subjectively*. The question is the *objective logic* of class relations in love.
Jan. 17, 1915.

Dear friend:

Please forgive the delay in replying to your letter. I wanted to reply yesterday but, being detained, had no time to write.

As regards the pamphlet draft, I found that the "demand for free love" was unclear, and that independent of your will or desire (which point I underlined when I said—the question is one of objective class relations and not a question of your subjective desires)--the demand will appear in contemporary social conditions a bourgeois and not a proletarian demand. You do not agree. All right. Let's study the matter once again.

Concretely: I listed 10 *possible* interpretations (interpretations inevitable in conditions of class struggle) and I commented that interpretations 1 to 7 would, in my opinion, be typical or characteristic for working class women and 8 to 10 for bourgeois women. If this is to be denied, you must show:

  (1) that the interpretations are false (then you must find others to take their place or reject the false ones);
  (2) that they are incomplete (therefore complete them);
  (3) or that they cannot be divided into proletarian and bourgeois interpretations. But you do not do any of these things.

You don't touch on points 1 to 7. I therefore assume that you recognize their correctness (in general)? What you write about the prostitution of women workers and their dependence, "the impossibility of saying no," is well within points 1

to 7. On this question there is no disagreement whatever
between us. You do not deny either that this is a *proletarian*
interpretation. That leaves us points 8 to 10.

You do not entirely "understand them" and you "object"
—"I do not understand how one *can* (these are your words)
identify (? ? ! !) free love with point 10." It turns out that
I "identify" and you are getting ready to rebuke and crush
me. What does this mean?

Bourgeois women understand by free love points 8 to 10—
that is my thesis. Do you deny this? Tell me then what bourgeois ladies understand by free love? You do not tell me. Do
not both literature and life *prove* that bourgeois women
understand free love precisely thus? They fully prove this!
You admit this by your silence. And since this is the case,
arising from the class position of these women, it would be
both impossible and naïve to "deny" this.

One must make a clear demarcation line and then coun-
terpose the proletarian standpoint. It is necessary to take into
consideration the objective fact that, otherwise, *without such
an approach, they* will extract the relevant passages from
your pamphlet, interpret them in their own way, your pamphlet will serve as grist to their mill; they will distort your
thoughts before the workers, sowing confusion among the
workers, awakening in them the fear that *you* have perhaps
brought them ideas *alien* to them. And in the hands of these
women are the gross (crass) newspapers and so on.

And you, completely abandoning the objective and class
standpoint, "attack" *me*, accuse me of identifying free love
with points 8 to 10. Astounding, simply astounding. . . .

"Even fleeting passion, a passing liaison" is "more poetic
and pure" than the "loveless kisses" exchanged as a matter
of habit between husband and wife. That is what you write.
And you propose writing this in your pamphlet. Excellent.
Is this counterposing logical?

Loveless kisses which a husband and wife exchange as a
matter of habit are *impure*. Agreed. What do you want to
make the contrary? A loving kiss, it would appear. No. You
make the contrary a "passing" (why passing?) "passion" (why

not love?). It follows logically that these loveless kisses (since they are passing) are the contrary of loveless kisses exchanged between husband and wife . . . strange!

Would it not be better in a popular pamphlet to counter-pose a proletarian civil marriage with love (adding, *if you simply must,* that a transient liaison or passion may be vile or pure), to loveless, vile and impure petty bourgeois, intel-lectual or peasant marriage? (See points 6 or 5 in my note.)

You place in opposition to one another not class *types* but cases, which might indeed arise. But is the matter one of cases? If you take as your subject-matter the individual case of impure kisses in marriage and pure kisses in a transient liaison, it is subject-matter for a novel (since a novel carries descriptions of *individuals,* analysis of character, psychology of *given* types)—but in a pamphlet?

You have grasped excellently my thought on the unsuitable quotation from Key* in saying that it is "stupid" to assume the role of a qualified "professor of love." True. And what about assuming the role of "professor of transient love"?

I do not want to engage in polemics. I would much rather have put this letter aside and waited for our next meeting. But I want the pamphlet to be good and I want no one to be able to draw any unpleasant phrases from it for you (a *single* phrase sometimes has the effect of a spoonful of tar), so that *no one can* put into your mouth words that you did *not want to say.*

I am sure that what you have written has been done "with-out meaning to," and I am sending this letter to you simply so that you can study your plan more thoroughly as a result of my letters, which is rather better than at the end of a conversation, for the plan is a very important thing.

Don't you know any French socialist woman? Translate to her (as if translating from the English) my points 1 to 10 and your remarks on "transient" love and so on. Watch her and listen attentively to her: it is a little experience to know what

---

* Ellen Key, Swedish woman of letters (1849-1926), who wrote on women's questions and child education and who defended the cause of the workers.

outside people think of things, what their impressions will be and what they expect of the pamphlet.
Jan. 24, 1915

Lenin, "Two Letters to Inessa Armand."

3. SEX AND BOURGEOIS MORALITY

"The extension of Freudian hypotheses seems 'educated,' even scientic, but it is ignorant, bungling. Freudian theory is the modern fashion. I mistrust the sexual theories of the articles, dissertations, pamphlets, etc., in short, of that particular kind of literature which flourishes luxuriantly in the dirty soil of bourgeois society. I mistrust those who are always contemplating the several questions, like the Indian saint his navel. It seems to me that these flourishing sexual theories which are mainly hypothetical, and often quite arbitrary hypotheses, arise from the personal need to justify personal abnormality or hypertrophy in sexual life before bourgeois morality, and to entreat its patience. This masked respect for bourgeois morality seems to me just as repulsive as poking about in sexual matters. However wild and revolutionary the behavior may be, it is still really quite bourgeois. It is, mainly, a hobby of the intellectuals and of the sections nearest them. There is no place for it in the Communist Party, in the class-conscious, fighting proletariat. . . .

"Young people, particularly, need the joy and force of life. Healthy sport, swimming, racing, walking, bodily exercises of every kind, and many-sided intellectual interests. Learning, studying, inquiry, as far as possible in common. That will give young people more than eternal theories and discussions about sexual problems and the so-called 'living to the full.' Healthy bodies, healthy minds! . . .

"The revolution demands concentration, increase of forces. From the masses, from individuals. It cannot tolerate orgiastic conditions, such as are normal for the decadent heroes and heroines of D'Annunzio. Dissoluteness in sexual life is bourgeois, is a phenomenon of decay. The proletariat is a rising class. It doesn't need intoxication as a narcotic or a stimulus. Intoxication as little by sexual exaggeration as by alcohol. It must not and shall not forget, forget the shame, the filth, the savagery of capitalism. It receives the strongest urge to fight from a class situation, from the communist ideal. It needs clarity, clarity, and again clarity. And so I repeat, no weakening, no waste, no destruction of forces. Self-control, self-discipline is not slavery, not even in love."

Clara Zetkin, *Lenin on the Woman Question.*

4. THE RIGHT TO DIVORCE

. . . This question of divorce is a striking illustration of the fact that one cannot be a democrat and a socialist without immediately demanding full freedom of divorce, for the absence of such freedom is an additional burden on the oppressed sex, woman—although it is not at all difficult to understand that the recognition of the *right* of women to leave their husbands is not an *invitation* to all wives to do so! . . .

Under capitalism it is usually the case, and not the exception, that the oppressed classes cannot "exercise" their democratic rights. In most cases the right to divorce is not exercised under capitalism, because the oppressed sex is crushed economically; because, no matter how democratic the state may be, the woman remains a "domestic slave" under capitalism, a slave of the bedroom, nursery, and kitchen. The right to elect "our" judges, public officials, teachers, jurors, etc., cannot be exercised under capitalism, in the majority of cases, because the workers and peasants are economically downtrodden. The same is true of a democratic republic. Our program "proclaims" the republic as "the sovereignty of the people," although every Social-Democrat knows perfectly well that under capitalism the most democratic republic leads merely to the bribery of the officials by the bourgeoisie and to an alliance between the Stock Exchange and the government.

Only those who are totally incapable of thinking, or those who are entirely unfamiliar with Marxism, will conclude that, therefore, a republic is of no use, that freedom of divorce is of no use, that democracy is of no use, that self-determination of nations is of no use! Marxists know that democracy does *not* abolish class oppression, but only makes the class struggle clearer, broader, more open and sharper; and this is what we want. The more complete freedom of divorce is, the clearer will it be to the woman that the source of her "domestic slavery" is not the lack of rights, but capitalism. The more democratic the system of government is, the clearer it will be to the workers that the root of the evil is not the lack of rights, but capitalism. The more complete national equality is (and it is *not* complete without freedom of secession), the clearer will it be to the workers of the oppressed nation that it is not a question of lack of rights, but of capitalism. And so on. . . .

The right to divorce, like *all* democratic rights under capitalism without exception, is difficult to exercise, is conventional, restricted, formal, and narrow. Nevertheless, no respectable Social-Democrat would consider any one who repudiated this right a democrat, let alone a socialist. This is the whole point. "Democracy" is nothing but the proclaiming and exercising of "rights" that are very little and very conventionally exercised under capitalism. But unless these rights are proclaimed, unless a struggle for immediate rights is waged, unless the masses are educated in the spirit of such a struggle, socialism is *impossible*.

Lenin, *Collected Works.*

5. THE WORKING CLASS AND NEO-MALTHUSIANISM

The question of abortion, that is, artificially induced miscarriages, evoked great interest and called forth many debates at the Pirogov Medical Congress. The reporter Luchkus presented data showing widespread practice of abortion in so-called civilized countries. There were eighty thousand abortions in New York in a year, and 36,000 in a month in France In St. Petersburg the percentage of abortions doubled in the last five years.

The Pirogov Medical Congress decided that mothers should not be criminally prosecuted for abortions and that doctors should be prosecuted only if they perform abortions for "pecuniary interests."

The majority at the congress, while arguing against punishment for abortions, naturally touched upon the question of neo-Malthusianism (birth control) as well as the social side of the problem. For instance, M. Vigdorchik, according to the report in the *Russkoye Slovo* (*Russian Word*), declared that one must "welcome contraceptive methods" while M. Astrakhan exclaimed, amid a storm of applause: "We are obliged to persuade mothers to give birth to children so that they may be crippled in educational institutions, so that they may be drafted for military service, so that they may be driven to suicide." ...

"To give birth to children so that they may be crippled." ... Only for this? Why not so that they may fight better, with greater solidarity, with greater consciousness and decisiveness, against the prevailing conditions of existence which are mutilating and destroying our generation?

Here we have the basic difference between the psychology of the peasant, the artisan, and the intellectual, of the petty-bourgeois generally, and the worker. The petty bourgeois sees and feels that he is perishing, that life is becoming more difficult, the struggle for existence more intolerable, that his own situation and that of his family more and more hopeless. This is an undeniable fact. And the petty bourgeois protests against it.

But *how* is he protesting?

He is protesting as the representative of a class destined to perish, despairing of its future, beaten and cowardly. The cry of the petty bourgeois is: Nothing can be done about it, so let there be fewer children to suffer our misfortunes and "hard labor," our poverty and humiliation.

The class-conscious worker is far removed from such a point of view. He will not allow his consciousness to be obscured by such cries, no matter how sincerely and feelingly they may be uttered. Yes, we workers and small owners, too, lead an unbearable life, filled with oppression and suffering. Our generation has fared worse than our fathers. But in one respect we are better off than our parents. *We have learned and are learning fast to struggle*—and to struggle not singly as the best of our fathers fought, not in the name of petty bourgeois slogans alien to us, but in the name of our own slogans, the slogans of our class. We are fighting better than our fathers did. Our children will fight still better, and *they will win. . . .*

This—and this alone—is why we are the absolute enemies of neo-Malthusianism, this tendency of the philistine couple, hardened and egotistical, who mumble in fright: "We shall somehow hang on, with God's help, but better not think about children."

Certainly, this does not prevent us from demanding the complete abolition of all laws prohibiting abortion or the distribution of medical information on birth control. etc. These laws only expose the hypocrisy of the ruling classes. These laws do not cure the diseases of capitalism, but make them especially deadly and grave for the oppressed masses. The freedom of medical information and the defense of the elementary democratic rights of men and women citizens is one thing. The social theory of neo-Malthusianism is something else. Class-conscious workers will always lead the most relentless struggle against any attempt to fasten this reactionary and cowardly teaching upon the class which is most advanced, most powerful, and best prepared for great social changes.

Lenin. *Collected Works.*

VII. Women in Socialist Construction

1. BUILDERS OF SOCIALISM

We must note as a pleasing fact and as an indication of the progress of culture in the rural districts the increased activity of the women collective farmers in social and organizational work. We know, for example, that about 6,000 women collective farmers are chairmen of collective farms, more than 60,000 are members of management boards of collective farms, 28,000 are group leaders, 100,000 are branch organizers, 9,000 are managers of collective farm dairies, and 7,000 are tractor drivers. Needless to say, these figures are incomplete; but even these figures are sufficient to indicate the great progress of culture in the rural districts. This fact, comrades, is of tremendous significance. It is of tremendous significance because women represent half the population of our country; they represent a huge army of workers; and they are called upon to bring up our children, our future generation, that is to say, our future. That is why we must not permit this huge army of working people to linger in darkness and ignorance! That is why we must welcome the growing social activity of the working women and their promotion to leading posts as an indubitable indication of the growth of our culture.

Stalin, *Selected Writings*.

2. PEOPLE AND TECHNIQUE

But modern technique alone will not carry you very far. You may have first-class technique, first-class mills and factories, but if you have not the people capable of harnessing that technique, you will find that your technique is just bare technique. For modern technique to produce results, people are required, cadres of working men and women capable of taking charge of the technique and advancing it.

The birth and growth of the Stakhanov movement means that such cadres have already appeared among the working men and women of our country. Some two years ago the party declared that in building new mills and factories and supplying our enterprises with modern machinery, we had performed only half the job. The party then declared that enthusiasm for the construction of new factories must be supplemented by enthusiasm for mastering these factories, that only in this way could the job be completed. It is obvious that the mastering of this new technique and the growth of new cadres have been proceeding during these two years. It is now clear that we already have such cadres. It is obvious, that without such cadres, without these new people, we would never have had a Stakhanov movement. Hence the new people, working men and women, who have mastered the new technique constitute the force that has shaped and advanced the Stakhanov movement.

Such are the conditions that gave rise to and advanced the Stakhanov movement.

Stalin, *Selected Writings.*

3. WOMEN ON THE COLLECTIVE FARMS

Now a few words about the *women,* the *women collective farmers.* The woman question in the collective farms is a big question, comrades. I know that many of you underrate the women and even laugh at them. That is a mistake, comrades, a serious mistake. The point is not only that women comprise half the population. Primarily, the point is that the collective farm movement has advanced a number of remarkable and capable women to leading positions. Look at this Congress, at the delegates, and you will realize that women have long since advanced from the ranks of the backward to the ranks of the forward. The women in the collective farms are a great force. To keep this force down would be criminal. It is our duty to bring the women in the collective farms forward and to make use of this great force.

Of course, not so long ago, the Soviet government had a slight misunderstanding with the women collective farmers. That was over the cow. But now this business about the cow has been settled, and the misunderstanding has been removed. We have reached the position where the majority of the collective farm households have a cow each. Another year or two will pass and there will not be a single collective farmer who will not have his own cow. We Bolsheviks will see to it that every one of our collective farmers has a cow.

As for the women collective farmers themselves, they must remember the power and significance of the collective farms for women; they must remember that only in the collective farm do they have the opportunity of becoming equal with men. Without collective farms—inequality; in collective farms—equal rights. Let our comrades, the women collective farmers, remember this and let them cherish the collective farm system as the apple of their eye.

Stalin, *Selected Writings.*

4. WOMEN IN THE PATRIOTIC WAR

Invaluable services in the cause of defense of the Motherland have been rendered by Soviet women, who work self-sacrificingly in the interests of the front, courageously bear all wartime hardships and inspire to fighting exploits the soldiers of the Red Army—the liberators of our Motherland.

The Patriotic War has shown that the Soviet people is capable of performing miracles and emerging victorious from the hardest trials. The workers, collective farmers, Soviet intellectuals, the whole Soviet people, are filled with determination to hasten the defeat of the enemy, to restore completely the economy ruined by the fascists, to make our country still stronger and more prosperous.

Stalin, *The Great Patriotic War.*

APPENDIX

Clara Zetkin was one of the outstanding figures in the international socialist and communist movement. A friend of Frederick Engels, a co-worker of Wilhelm Liebknecht and August Bebel in Germany, she was the foremost leader of the socialist women in the struggles for women's rights both in Germany and internationally. Together with Wilhelm Pieck, now president of the German Democratic Republic, and with Rosa Luxemburg and Karl Liebknecht, she helped to found the Communist Party of Germany. She and Lenin had their famous conversations on the woman question (given in part below and on page 80) in 1920. She later included the full discussion in her pamphlet, Lenin on the Woman Question.

"The thesis must clearly point out that real freedom for women is possible only through communism. The inseparable connection between the social and human position of the woman, and private property in the means of production, must be strongly brought out. That will draw a clear and ineradicable line of distinction between our policy and feminism. And it will also supply the basis for regarding the woman question as a part of the social question, of the workers' problem, and so bind it firmly to the proletarian class struggle and the revolution. The Communist women's movement must itself be a mass movement, a part of the general mass movement. Not only of the proletariat, but of all the exploited and oppressed, all the victims of capitalism or any other mastery. In that lies its significance for the class struggles of the proletariat and for its historical creation—communist society. . . . We must win over to our side the millions of toiling women in the towns and villages. Win them for our struggles and in particular for the communist trans-

89

formation of society. There can be no real mass movement without women.

"Our ideological conceptions give rise to principles of organization. No special organizations for women. A woman Communist is a member of the party just as a man Communist, with equal rights and duties. There can be no difference of opinion on that score. Nevertheless, we must not close our eyes to the fact that the party must have bodies, working groups, commissions, committees, bureaus or whatever you like, whose particular duty it is to arouse the masses of women workers, to bring them into contact with the party, and to keep them under its influence. That, of course, involves systematic work among them. We must train those whom we arouse and win, and equip them for the proletarian class struggle under the leadership of the Communist Party. I am thinking not only of proletarian women. whether they work in the factory or at home. The poor peasant women, the petty bourgeois—they, too, are the prey of capitalism, and more so than ever since the war. The unpolitical, unsocial, backward psychology of these women, their isolated sphere of activity, the entire manner of their life—these are facts. It would be absurd to overlook them, absolutely absurd. We need appropriate bodies to carry on work amongst them, special methods of agitation and forms of organization. That is not feminism, that is practical, revolutionary expediency. . . .

"That is why it is right for us to put forward demands favorable to women. This is not a minimum, a reform program in the sense of the Social-Democrats, of the Second International. It is not a recognition that we believe in the eternal character, or even in the long duration of the rule of the bourgeoisie and their state. It is not an attempt to appease women by reforms and to divert them from the path of revolutionary struggle. It is not that nor any other reformist swindle. Our demands are practical conclusions which we have drawn from the burning needs, the shameful humiliation of women in bourgeois society, defenseless and without rights. We demonstrate thereby that we recognize these needs, and are aware of the humiliation of the woman, the privileges of the man. That we hate, yes, hate everything, and will abolish everything which tortures and oppresses the woman worker, the housewife, the peasant woman, the wife of the petty trader, yes, and in many cases the women of the possessing classes. The rights and social regulations which we demand for women from bourgeois society show that we understand the position and interests of women, and will have consideration for them under the proletarian dictatorship. Not, of course, as the reformists do, lulling them to inaction and keeping them on leading strings. No, of course not; but as revolutionaries who call upon the women to work as equals in transforming the old economy and ideology.' . . .

"Every such struggle brings us in opposition to respectable bourgeois relationships, and to their not less respectable reformist admirers whom it compels, either to fight together with us under our leadership—which they don't want to do—or to be shown up in their true colors. That is, the struggle clearly brings out the differences between us and other parties, brings out our communism. It wins us the confidence of the masses of women who feel themselves exploited, enslaved, suppressed, by the domination of the man, by the power of the employer, by the whole of bourgeois society. Betrayed and deserted by all, the working women will recognize that they must fight together with us.

"Must I again swear to you, or let you swear, that the struggles for our demands for women must be bound up with the object of seizing power, of establishing the proletarian dictatorship? That is our Alpha and Omega at the present time. That is clear, quite clear. But the women of the working class will not feel irresistibly driven into sharing our struggles for the state power if we only and always put forward that one demand, though it were with the trumpets of Jericho. No, no! The women must be made conscious of the political connection between our demands and their own suffering, needs, and wishes. They must realize what the proletarian dictatorship means for them: complete equality with man in law and practice, in the family, in the state, in society; an end to the power of the bourgeoisie."

"Soviet Russia shows that," I interrupted.

"That will be the great example in our teaching," Lenin continued. "Soviet Russia puts our demands for women in a new light. Under the proletarian dictatorship those demands are not objects of struggle between the proletariat and the bourgeoisie. They are part of the structure of communist society. That indicates to women in other countries the decisive importance of the winning of power by the proletariat. The difference must be sharply emphasized, so as to get the women into the revolutionary class struggle of the proletariat. It is essential for the Communist parties, and for their triumph, to rally them on a clear understanding of principle and a firm organizational basis. But don't let us deceive ourselves. Our national sections still lack a correct understanding of this matter. They are standing idly by while there is this task of creating a mass movement of working women under Communist leadership. They don't understand that the development and management of such a mass movement is an important part of entire party activity, indeed, a half of general party work. Their occasional recognition of the necessity and value of a powerful, clear-headed Communist women's movement is a platonic verbal recognition, not the constant care and obligation of the party.

"Agitation and propaganda work among women, their awakening and revolutionization, is regarded as an incidental matter, as an affair which only concerns women comrades. They alone are reproached because work in that direction does not proceed more quickly and more vigorously. That is wrong, quite wrong! Real separatism and as the French say, feminism *à la rebours,* feminism upside down! What is at the basis of the incorrect attitude of our national sections? In the final analysis it is nothing but an under-estimation of woman and her work. Yes, indeed! Unfortunately it is still true to say of many of our comrades, 'scratch a Communist and find a Philistine.' Of course, you must scratch the sensitive spot, their mentality as regards woman. Could there be a more damning proof of this than the callous acquiescence of men who see how women grow worn out in the petty, monotonous household work, their strength and time dissipated and wasted, their minds growing narrow and stale, their hearts beating slowly, their will weakened? Of course, I am not speaking of the ladies of the bourgeoisie who shove onto servants the responsibility for all household work, including the care of children. What I am saying applies to the overwhelming majority of women, to the wives of workers and to those who stand all day in a factory.

"So few men—even among the proletariat—realize how much effort and trouble they could save women, even quite do away with, if they were to lend a hand in 'woman's work. But no, that is contrary to the 'right and dignity of a man.' They want their peace and comfort. The home life of the woman is a daily sacrifice to a thousand unimportant trivialities. The old master right of the man still lives in secret. His slave takes her revenge, also secretly. The backwardness of women, their lack of understanding for the revolutionary ideals of the man decrease his joy and determination in fighting. They are like little worms which, unseen, slowly but surely, rot and corrode. I know the life of the worker, and not only from books. Our Communist work among the women, our political work, embraces a great deal of educational work among men. We must root out the old 'master' idea to its last and smallest root, in the party and among the masses. That is one of our political tasks, just as is the urgently necessary task of forming a staff of men and women comrades, well trained in theory and practice, to carry on party activity among working women."

To my question about the conditions in Soviet Russia on this point, Lenin replied:

"The government of the proletarian dictatorship, together with the Communist Party and trade unions, is of course leaving no stone unturned in the effort to overcome the backward ideas of men and women, to destroy the old un-

Communist psychology. In law there is naturally complete equality of rights for men and women. And everywhere there is evidence of a sincere wish to put this equality into practice. We are bringing the women into the social economy, into legislation and government. All educational institutions are open to them, so that they can increase their professional and social capacities. We are establishing communal kitchens and public eating-houses, laundries and repair shops, infant asylums, kindergartens, children's homes, educational institutes of all kinds. In short, we are seriously carrying out the demand in our program for the transference of the economic and educational functions of the separate household to society. That will mean freedom for the women from the old household drudgery and dependence on man. That enables her to exercise to the full her talents and her inclinations. The children are brought up under more favorable conditions than at home. We have the most advanced protective laws for women workers in the world, and the officials of the organized workers carry them out. We are establishing maternity hospitals, homes for mothers and children, mothercraft clinics, organizing lecture courses on child care, exhibitions teaching mothers how to look after themselves and their children, and similar things. We are making the most serious efforts to maintain women who are unemployed and unprovided for.

"We realize clearly that that is not very much, in comparison with the needs of the working women, that it is far from being all that is required for their real freedom. But still it is tremendous progress, as against conditions in tsarist-capitalist Russia. It is even a great deal compared with conditions in countries where capitalism still has a free hand. It is a good beginning in the right direction, and we shall develop it further. With all our energy, you may believe that. For every day of the existence of the Soviet state proves more clearly that we cannot go forward without the women."

BIBLIOGRAPHY OF SOURCES

Chapter I

1. Joseph Stalin, *Anarchism or Socialism?* New York, 1951.
   Frederick Engels, *The Origin of the Family, Private Property, and the State*, pp. 146-48, New York, 1942.
2. *Ibid.*, pp. 41-43.
3. *Ibid.*, pp. 47-50.
4. *Ibid.*, pp. 54-62.

Chapter II

1. Karl Marx, *Capital*, Vol. I, pp. 239-40, International Publishers ed., New York, 1947.
2. *Ibid.*, pp. 390-91.
3. *Ibid.*, pp. 391-92.
3. *Ibid.*, pp. 495-96.
4. Frederick Engels, *Condition of the Working Class in England in 1844*, p. 141. London, 1950.
   Ibid., pp. 142-44.
   Ibid., pp. 129-30.

Chapter III

1. Karl Marx and Frederick Engels, *The Communist Manifesto*, pp. 26-28, New York, 1948.
2. Frederick Engels, *The Origin of the Family, Private Property, and the State*, pp. 62-66.
3. V. I. Lenin, *Women and Society*, pp. 30-31, New York, 1938 ("The Fifth International Congress for Combatting Prostitution," *Rabochaya Pravda*, July 26, 1913).

Chapter IV

1. V. I. Lenin *Letters from Afar*, p. 31, New York, 1932.
   V. I. Lenin, *Women and Society*, pp. 11-13 (Speech at the First All-Russian Congress of Women Workers, Nov. 19, 1918).
2. Marx-Engels-Lenin Institute, *Joseph Stalin: A Political Biography*, pp. 65-66, New York, 1949 ("International Women's Day," 1925).
3. V. I. Lenin, *Women and Society*, pp. 27-29 ("International Women's Day," *Pravda*, March 8, 1921).

Chapter V

1. Constitution of the U.S.S.R., Article 122.
   Joseph Stalin, *Selected Writings*, pp. 388-89, New York, 1942 ("Report on the Draft Constitution of the U.S.S.R.," Nov. 25, 1936).
2. V. I. Lenin, *Women and Society*, pp. 15-20 ("The Tasks of the Working Women's Movement in the Soviet Republic," Sept. 23, 1919).
3. *Ibid.*, pp. 13-15 ("A Great Beginning," June 28, 1919).

4. *Ibid.*, pp. 21-24 ("Soviet Power and the Position of Women," *Pravda,* Nov. 6, 1919).

5. *Ibid.*, pp. 25-26 ("To Women Workers," Feb. 21, 1920).

6. *Ibid.*, pp. 26-27 ("International Women's Day," *Pravda*, March 7, 1920).

7. Joseph Stalin, *Collected Works*, Vol. V, Russian ed., pp. 349-51 ("On the 5th Anniversary of the First Congress of Working and Peasant Women," *Communist Woman*, Nov. 1923).

Chapter VI

1. Frederick Engels, *The Origin of the Family, Private Property, and the State*, pp. 63-73.

2. V. I. Lenin, "Two Letters to Inessa Armand, Jan. 17 and 24, 1915," *Bolshevik*, No. 13, pp. 58-63, Moscow, July 1939.

3. Clara Zetkin, *Lenin on the Woman Question*, pp. 7, 12-13, New York, 1934.

4. V. I. Lenin, *Collected Works*, Vol. XIX, pp. 259-61, New York, 1942 ("A Caricature of Marxism," Oct. 1916).

5. V. I. Lenin, *Collected Works*, Vol. XVI, second Russian ed., pp. 497-99 ("The Working Class and Neo-Malthusianism," *Pravda*, June 29, 1913).

Chapter VII

1. Joseph Stalin, *Selected Writings*, p. 334 ("Report to 17th Party Congress," 1934).

2. *Ibid.*, p. 373 (Speech at the First All-Union Conference of Stakhanovites, Nov. 17, 1935).

3. *Ibid.*, p. 294 (Speech at the Joint All-Union Conference of Collective Farm Shock Workers, Feb. 19, 1933).

4. Joseph Stalin, *The Great Patriotic War of the Soviet Union*, p. 123, New York, 1945.

Appendix

Clara Zetkin, *Lenin on the Woman Question*, pp. 14-20.